Forgotten Tales of
Kentucky

Keven McQueen
Illustrations by Kyle McQueen

Charleston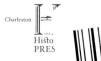
THE
Histo
PRES

Published by The History Press
Charleston, SC 29403
www.historypress.net

First published 2008

Manufactured in the United States

ISBN 978.1.59629.534.6

Library of Congress Cataloging-in-Publication Data

McQueen, Keven.
Forgotten tales of Kentucky / Keven McQueen.
p. cm.
Includes bibliographical references.
ISBN 978-1-59629-534-6
1. Tales--Kentucky. 2. Legends--Kentucky. 3. Folklore--Kentucky. I.
Title.
GR110.K4M37 2008
398.209769--dc22
                          2008033420

Contents

Introduction

What! Back for more strange yarns from Kentucky's past, are you?

Unlike its predecessor, *The Kentucky Book of the Dead*, there are practically no ghost stories in this book.

However, there are accounts of more earthbound (though equally mysterious) incidents, all rescued from oblivion through the magic of backbreaking research. One chapter describes a variety of monsters, all exceedingly unattractive, that petrified our ancestors. Another chapter lists several occasions on which the skeletons of members of some long-forgotten race of gigantic humans were found. A couple of chapters describe unpleasant rainfalls of exotic substances ranging from bloody meat to knitting needles to rocks. Some of our fortunate forebears stumbled across hidden treasure; their triumphs are recounted. And if the graveyard lore from *The Kentucky Book of the Dead* is your sort of thing, you will find plenty more of the same herein.

As ever, useful bits of Kentucky history are nestled among these bizarre tales. Read and believe; or, read and disbelieve. I just hope you have a good time in either case.

Kentucky Monsters

Nepal has the Yeti; the Pacific Northwestern United States has Sasquatch; and Scotland has the Loch Ness Monster. Kentucky has been home to, well, quite a number of unlovely homegrown monsters. All of them seem to be either extinct or very good at hiding, as no one has seen them in a number of years—at least, no one who has lived to tell about it.

The 1795 *Kentucky Almanac*, published in Lexington by John Bradford, included an account of a bizarre creature seen on Cove Creek in the Cumberland Mountains by members of Captain John Baird's mounted infantry: "[I]t had only two legs, and stood almost upright, covered with scales of a black, brown and light yellow color, in spots like rings, a white tuft or crown on the top of its head, about four feet high, with a head as big as a two pound stone and large eyes of a firey [*sic*] red." The animal did not run, but struck a "daring posture" and stared at the men. One soldier, Ensign McDonald, took the initiative to strike it with a sword. It leapt eight feet vertically, expelling from its mouth a substance that appeared to be blood. The animal fled to a laurel thicket, leaving large goose-like tracks, but it showed a disposition to stop and fight as it ran. The local Indians were familiar with the creature and claimed that its breath meant certain death. The only cure was to immediately immerse oneself in water. The account of the monster was reproduced in *Clark's 2006 Kentucky Almanac*.

Allensville, in Todd County, was visited several times in summer 1882 by a prodigy that killed dogs and then ate only their heads. The one description we have of the thing is that it was "considerably larger than a good-sized dog," which does not tell us much. Perhaps it was the same creature that troubled the residents of Boyle County starting in 1883. This one was seen by witnesses in daylight and, like the Allensville monster, it was described as being "as large as a dog and much longer." Some theorized that it was a jaguar or a tiger. Whatever it was, in January 1885, it ate the greater portion of a dog tied up in C.K. Elder's kennel. As a result of such deeds, the monster was dubbed "the Dog Eater" by the press and by March 1885 it reportedly was devouring the hounds over in Marion County. Many frightening stories about the Dog Eater circulated, some more believable than others. It was said that whenever the monster couldn't find a tasty Old Shep, it would settle for horses, sheep, geese, ducks or even people. Allegedly, a human arm was found in the woods of Boyle County after one of the Dog Eater's raids, but the *Danville Advocate* called it a "false report." After spending a few happy years consuming canines and terrifying the populace, the Dog Eater disappeared and was never heard from again—at least in that neck of the woods.

In spring 1909, "bloodcurdling" cries issued nightly from the woods near Switzer, Franklin County. People compared it to the sound of someone calling hogs, but with a "wailing tremor." Generally, the sounds began around 7:00 p.m. and continued until 2:00 or 3:00 a.m. and some witnesses claimed that they had heard the sounds off and on for nearly a decade, which would indicate that the culprit, if human, was one very persistent, very insane hog-calling insomniac. Many well-known residents heard the sound, including Berry, Henry and Jeff Hockensmith; Jennie, Charlie and John Hart; and Joseph Newman. Locals favored two theories: that the legendary Dog Eater had moved to Franklin County, or that some wild animal must have escaped from the circus and was hiding in the woods.

In August 1882, the skull of an animal was found in Owenton, Owen County. It resembled something from an H.R. Giger painting and nothing in the zoological annals. Whatever the monstrosity was, it had multiple rows of teeth, no eye sockets, no brainpan, no attachment for a spinal column and two bony protrusions resembling ears. Another strange skull was brought to the *Richmond Herald* office in late 1882 by Captain A.J. Mershon, who claimed to have found it in the mountains of Harlan County. The cranium resembled that of a human, except for its length, its unusually sloping brow and the fact that it sported a set of horns.

A group of Scott County boys were exploring the caves on a cliff overlooking Elkhorn Creek in October 1884 when they caught a large bird of unprecedented description. Its wings, tail, thighs, legs and feet resembled those of an owl, but its face was longer than a baboon's and it had a large, human-like lower jaw. Its head and neck were covered with down; in fact, the hair growing around its jaw made one observer think it resembled a tiny man with mutton-chop whiskers. Its small eyes were located near the center of its face, like a human or an owl. Its temperament varied from extreme lethargy to extreme fierceness. The bird was owned by Pres T. Pullen of Georgetown, who toyed with the idea of placing it on display at the Cincinnati Zoological Garden. There is no evidence that Pullen carried out his plan.

The lonesome road that led from Uptonville—a town located in both Larue and Hardin Counties—to Millerstown, Grayson County, was not a pleasant place to be at night in autumn 1884. On several occasions, wary travelers were petrified by a boojum that would emerge from the dark woods and chase people home. Jake Vance, who lived near Uptonville, was the only witness known to have seen the animal in the daytime. He described it as being twice the size of a wildcat and covered with black and white spots.

A strange-looking critter was spotted on the farm of Roy Arnold in Bryantsville, Garrard County, in June 1887. Arnold's son described it as yellow, three feet long, short-legged, and the proud owner of a long, bushy tail and a mouthful of teeth nearly a foot long. The boy shot at it, but missed.

In November 1887, the *Henderson Journal* described a peculiar eyesore that had been shot near a Webster County creek. It was a foot long, covered with black hair and had a long bushy appendage that was assumed to be a tail. It had a sharp, weasel-like snout and a white stripe running from the tip of its nose to its shoulder. The creature had two legs and presumably could walk upright, but the structure of its feet suggested that it lived in water. The animal was stuffed and put on display at Mayer's Hardware Store. Presumably, it now belongs to the ages.

In May 1888, a thing was killed near Augusta, Bracken County, that was two feet long, weighed twelve pounds, had a head and front feet like a squirrel's—but four times the size—and hind feet like a raccoon's. Its like had never been seen before and evidently never has since.

An aquatic "varmint" with the disagreeable habit of eating piglets, ducks, turkeys and chickens was killed by rabbit hunters near Lair Station, Harrison County, appropriately around Halloween 1889. The animal put up a heroic fight, singlehandedly whipping several hunting dogs and biting one hunter, Frank Conway, on the hand. It was four feet long and covered with shiny black fur. It had a long, tapering, weasel-like head with tiny ears, short forelegs, long hind legs and a short, broad, flat tail. Another hunter, Tom Snodgrass, expressed his intention to send the carcass to a taxidermist.

In 1894, the border of Mercer and Washington Counties was troubled by an ornery organism that raided henhouses and stole farm items such as eggs, milk, meat and even live pigs and lambs. At the end of April, Jack Agee spotted the culprit emerging from his springhouse. It was six and a half feet tall and had long white hair and a beard. Its legs were covered with hair and it wore a sheepskin loincloth. It had bear-like feet with long claws. Strangest of all, "a light came from his eyes and mouth similar to fire."

Agee's story was duly met with skepticism until May 2, when Joseph Ewalt's family found Ewalt lying unconscious near his springhouse. When he revived, he claimed that when he had opened the door, the man-beast described by Agee had come charging out. On the morning of May 6, Eph Boston and his sons Tom and James saw the creature heading for their barn "walking in a half-gallop, half-run."

Paralyzed with fear, they did not dare follow it. A few minutes later, it came out clutching three chickens. Tom Boston fired a shot at it, causing the monster to look back at the Bostons and then run away "swifter than a horse." They were able to keep up with its gait well enough to see it duck into a large cave near the mouth of Deep Creek.

Two days later, the Bostons, along with a half-dozen other men, went to the cave to seek the creature, no doubt in hopes of capturing and rehabilitating him. They found bones, animal skins and feathers scattered liberally about the cave's entrance. They also found two well-worn clubs, which they carried away as souvenirs of a memorable occasion. No one was willing to venture too far into the passage, especially after a loud, unearthly yell issued from the darkness. The men emerged from the cave as quickly as the laws of physics permitted and vowed they would come back soon and give the creature what-for. But there were no follow-up reports, so we must wonder about the outcome. Was the cave home to an authentic monster or just one of the many crazy "wild men" who populated the woods in those dear dead days—a wild man with bear-like feet and who could run like a horse? Or was it all just a journalistic hoax?

Starting in early June 1896, Greenup Countians' humdrum lives were made more interesting by a monster that killed and ate dogs, made off with chickens and, disturbingly, attempted to dig up graves. Several citizens saw it and were so scared that they took up arms and formed nightly patrols. A policeman named James Smith described it as being "as large as a shepherd dog, almost white in color with black spots." Officer Smith managed to shoot it on the night of June 16, but it took off yelping for the woods. Nervous folk said it must be some exotic animal that escaped from a traveling circus—the default rationalization people had back then when faced with a creature they could not explain.

In spring 1897, two Carroll County anglers, Charley Robinson and Dave Ward, caught a couple of uglies in the Ohio River. They were of the same species, though one was a foot long and the other eight inches. They were shaped liked eels but had "two short, weak legs" near their heads and two more near their tails. They appeared to be blind and had catfish-like heads, but their gills were entirely outside of their heads. For some time, they were on display at the firm of Driskell & Company in Ghent.

Dukedom, Graves County, was allegedly perturbed in August 1897 by an exotic being that weighed an estimated four hundred pounds, had walrus-like tusks and left in its wake footprints fifteen inches long and seven inches wide.

In March 1899, Milton West caught a singular fish at Pond River, eighteen miles north of Elkton, Todd County. It resembled a mackerel but sported a "fully-developed set of upper and lower teeth," long, sharp and squirrel-like. It was on exhibition in Elkton for several days.

A nocturnal creature called a "what-is-it" wandered the environs of Leitchfield, Grayson County, as summer 1899 drew to a close. It made itself obnoxious by feasting upon calves and other small animals and by eluding hunters. Unlike most such mysterious beasts, however, this one didn't just stay hidden in the woods. On the night of September 19, it sauntered into town, where many witnesses saw it in several locations, including an alley behind W.B. Hill's store. It was described as a long, black animal with pointed ears and a drooping tail. "It makes a large track, differing from a dog in size and heel projection," said the *Leitchfield Gazette*. Some people theorized that it was a wolf that had escaped from a western Kentucky circus. Remarked the *Gazette:* "[T]here is not so much wandering at night from the family fireside as there used to be…Just at present Leitchfield does not need a curfew law in the least, as the escaped animal answers the purpose admirably."

Scottsville, Allen County, was agitated in the summer of 1900 by a "dog-eating quadruped" that dwelled in a cave near the town. It was described as being long and tall, covered with gray hair, and possessing a lengthy tail with coils at the end. At last report, the worried citizens were organizing a posse to track down and kill the marauder.

Most of these outlandish Kentucky creatures dwelt in the lonesome forests where the woodbine twineth, but at least one made its appearance in the middle of a large industrial city. In July 1901, some workmen were digging at George Ritman's sand pits on the corner of Eleventh Street and St. Louis Avenue in Louisville when they "discovered a strange animal hiding in a burrowed hole." They coaxed it out with bread crumbs, then lassoed it. Nobody knew what it was, so Ritman took it to his home at 718 East Broadway. It had grayish-brown hair and seemed to combine various features of the opossum, the raccoon, the groundhog and the prairie dog. "It eats almost anything given to it," said the *Courier-Journal*, "but though voracious in appetite, it is not vicious in disposition. Mr. Ritman contemplates the purchase of an extensive library on animals with a view to learning the name of the What-is-it. In the meantime, the neighborhood is guessing." They appear to have guessed in vain, for there was no follow-up explanation. The fate of the friendly little creature, to say nothing of its genus, remains a mystery.

The *Pineville* (Bell County) *Herald* reported in June 1903 that long-clawed tracks six inches in length were left by a "monster wild beast" of unknown species that ruined Brantley Smith and John Wilson's fishing trip at Yellow Creek. Smith shot at it, but missed.

Frank Sedler and his family went camping in Boone County, on the Kentucky side of the Ohio River, on the night of July 22, 1903. Around midnight, he was awakened by screams issuing from his children's tent. Investigating, he saw his year-old baby "in the clutches of a creature apparently half human, half beast," as a newspaper report described it. When Sedler shouted, the varmint dropped the child and jumped into the river. Sedler theorized that it was a baboon that had escaped from a boat show.

Mercer County had some lively times in winter 1903 due to an unknown wild animal that considered it sport to eat dogs and chase lonesome travelers. In February, John Wigham was returning to his home in the hamlet of Nevada when he heard "a yelp similar to that made by an infuriated dog." Suddenly, he confronted a creature "larger than a

calf" with eyes that shone like fire. Wigham gave his horse a wholehearted lashing, not that it was probably necessary. The creature followed and gave chase for over two miles. It did not give up until Wigham was nearly home and it saw the lights of the village. Several fox hunters pursued the animal but their enthusiasm waned after several of their dogs were torn to fragments by the creature. Afterward, about a hundred Mercer Countians planned to enter the woods in pursuit of the animal, but the hunt was abandoned when no trace of it was found.

Kentucky's own version of the Loch Ness Monster was often seen in the early twentieth century, beginning circa 1902. The September 8, 1904 edition of the *Owensboro Messenger* alluded to a monster like a sea serpent that had caused people in the vicinity of Wright's Ferry to live "in fear and dread for the past two years." It dwelled in the pool between the Rumsey and Spottsville locks on the Green River and was said to resemble a large black horse, much like Nessie or the equine-headed oddity that allegedly dwells in Lake Champlain, Vermont. The size of the creature varied depending on who was telling the story. Some reported that it was merely as big as a house while others maintained that it was two hundred feet long. There were even reports that it came ashore at Wrightsburg, McLean County, to eat a horse. In summer 1904, passengers aboard a boat that had docked at Beech Grove, McLean County, saw the monster surface only about thirty feet from shore.

For a time, parents refused to allow their children to play near the Green River and men were reluctant to sail in small boats lest the monster capsize them. Their worst fears seemed confirmed when a thirteen-year-old boy named Ivo Lamb disappeared at Beech Grove while riding a small boat that followed a steamboat's wake. It was suspected that he drowned, but when his body did not surface, suspicions turned toward the monster. The *Owensboro Messenger* of October 21 bore the unsettling headline:

MYSTERY SURROUNDS DROWNING OF
BOY AT BEECH GROVE

*Residents of Neighborhood Believe His Body
Has Been Devoured by the "Marine Monster."*

A farmer named Wesley Luck, who helped drag the river for the body, stated that he had seen the monster in the river recently. The *Green River News* of Webster County soon ran an account, reprinted in the *Henderson Daily Gleaner*, stating that the monster actually attacked Luck and a man named Dave Knight as they searched for Ivo Lamb's body on a skiff: "[They] were forced to fight to save themselves from his vicious efforts to devour them." The *News* concluded: "[T]his animal, or fish…has become a serious menace to the peace and happiness of the community." Lamb's body eventually did turn up, drowned but not eaten, and he was buried in Onton, Webster County.

The leading theory at the time was that the Green River monster was a "sea horse" (an old-fashioned name for the hippopotamus) that—you guessed it—somehow escaped from a circus. Unlike most ephemeral monsters, however, this one might have left behind some proof of its existence. On September 7, 1904, when fear of the creature was reaching a crescendo, a fisherman named R.L. Hollingsworth found the blackened, but well-preserved, cap of the tooth of some gigantic animal. The cap was eight inches long, two inches high, four inches wide and "as hard as flint." It was placed on exhibition at Head's Drugstore in Owensboro. The present whereabouts of the relic are unknown.

Another Green River prodigy was active in the early 1940s in the vicinity of Houchin's Ferry, Edmonson County.

On the "Day Which Shall Live in Infamy," the *Courier-Journal* ran an article on recent sightings. Descriptions varied wildly; some residents claimed it was at least twelve feet long and weighed up to three hundred pounds. Many swore that it had a head resembling a catfish's, unlike the monster from the turn of the century, which was reported to have a head like a horse. It had a kittenish disposition and was known to splash around in the water—not a bemusing sight to boaters, who avoided it whenever possible. A ferryboat operator named Vertice Dossey claimed to have seen it many times and said he could always tell when it was coming because "it used to be preceded by hundreds of fish fleeing for their lives." Dossey added: "But now [the fish] ain't so many to scare. Either the monster has et [*sic*] them all or they have left for safer waters." Dossey denied

the obvious explanation—that the monster was a freakishly large catfish—stating that unlike a catfish it could leap out of the water. He colorfully described the monster:

> *It's got a powerful big head. It could swallow a man without no trouble. Once it opened its mouth and I got a glimpse inside. I could have rolled a barrel—and I don't mean a keg, I mean a big barrel—in its mouth. It's got fins and tail just like any fish and eyes as big as horse apples setting out of its head; it's got the longest whiskers or feelers you ever saw, and once when it jumped I thought I saw legs on its belly. But I can't rightly say about the legs.*

Another citizen, Lester Webb, theorized that the beast lived in one of the many unexplored underground streams in nearby Mammoth Cave. The creature has not been spotted in many a decade.

In March 1907, a farmhand named Jim Peters was laboring in Bowman's Woods, near High Bridge, a short distance from Buena Vista, Garrard County, when his dog wandered into a thicket. A short time later, the canine came running back to its master in a funk of fear. Peters found out why when a large, hairy humanoid came lumbering into the clearing, apparently in pursuit of the dog. The creature stopped within twenty yards of Peters, who stood frozen to the spot in terror. When Peters worked up the nerve to ask the strange visitor its business, it turned and left. Once Peters's legs were back in working order, he hurried to his employer, S.D. Scott, postmaster of

Buena Vista. Scott organized a search party, but the only trace they found were bare human footprints in the mud near a riverbank—tracks that featured "claw-like toenails." This is a contemporary description of what Peters saw:

> *The creature wore no clothes except a coon skin tied about its loins. Its long black hair streamed down its back and breast in a matted mass, and covered the face so that he could not see whether it had a beard or not. Its body was covered with a coat of soft, fuzzy black hair and its finger and toe nails were long and curved like talons.*

There is no evidence the creature was ever seen again. Some thought it was an escaped lunatic running wild in the woods; however, persons who are into this sort of thing will note that except for the detail about the demurely placed coonskin, the description sounds remarkably like the canonical depiction of Bigfoot.

In autumn 1909, a private graveyard used by the Jones and Williams families, who lived near the Kentucky River in Owen County, was visited by some creature whose motive appeared to be ghoulish vandalism rather than paying its respects. Something dug holes in the ground and raided the graves, leaving casket handles, pieces of wood and the departed strewn about. Some prosaic souls thought groundhogs were the culprits, while others pointed out that the holes were too large to have been made by said burrowing rodent, and it seems unlikely that groundhogs could pull bodies out of graves. (The reader will recall that in 1896, Greenup County was visited by some doglike being that also attempted to exhume bodies.) The cemetery was surrounded by a solid rock fence five feet high, which would seem an insurmountable obstacle to most animals. A reporter in Owenton commented: "There is an animal known as 'grave digger,' but if any of the species exists in this country, he has failed to show himself in the daytime."

Around 1888, Bohon, Mercer County, was terrorized by the "Crying Devil," a peculiar fowl so called because of its "unearthly and frightful cry." No one got a good look at it, but its nighttime screams made many a man reach with trembling hands for his Bible and/or shotgun. Eventually, the bird left for parts unknown and was largely forgotten, but it reappeared in September 1913 in the community of Ebenezer. It turned up on the farm of T.T. Dean, who said it was as large as a turkey gobbler and nocturnal. According to the *Harrodsburg Herald*, "[Dean] says it chills his blood and makes him feel like praying whenever he hears it, and so frightful is the noise that his dog, which was never known to fear anything, and the family cat run under the house and hide when the bird cries." Dean tried repeatedly to kill or capture his tormentor, but to no avail. In December, the bird got caught on a trot line's hook and drowned in the Kentucky River. It reportedly "resembled a huge duck," had a wingspan of five and a half feet, weighed twelve pounds and had three toes on each foot. W.M. Bunton had a taxidermist preserve and mount the once-proud Crying Devil and displayed it in his home. Perhaps the stuffed specimen still exists in someone's attic, awaiting the scrutiny of ornithologists. Apparently, the bizarre bird had no mate or offspring, for the community has remained untroubled by the Crying Devil's call—and let us be grateful for that.

In Martin County, the matriarch of the Turner family, "Maw" Turner, had an unenviable experience on her property many decades ago. To set the mood, her land was densely wooded and crowned with a cemetery on a hill. The church she attended was about a mile from her home. She walked to services and back, often in darkness made gloomier by the overhanging trees. One night, circa 1940, she was coming home from church. As she rounded a curve across from a sulfur spring, something six feet tall and covered with hair stepped out of the shadows and hugged her. Thinking her eldest son Carl was playing a prank, she gave the nameless thing a hug in return, whereupon it let go and ran away. Deonna Pinson, one of Maw's great-granddaughters, remarks: "Now, Maw Turner, who was only five feet and one inch tall, was a hard-headed widow who gave birth to twins two weeks after her husband was brutally murdered, so she wasn't flighty by a long shot. In fact, if ever there existed a soul with no imagination, it would be Maw." Maw returned home in high dudgeon, only to find Carl sitting in the living room with all her other children. "That weren't funny, Carl," she remonstrated. Carl had no idea what she was talking about and the other kids were quick to affirm that he had been in the house the whole time. Frightened, Carl suggested that the hugging bandit had been a bear. No, said Maw Turner, bears are not built like six-foot-tall hairy men. Besides, a bear can only stand upright for a few seconds at a time. Deonna Pinson writes:

> *Could it have been a neighbor playing a prank? Could have been, but the neighbors were few and far away. Could it have been one of her fellow churchgoers? Maybe, but he would have had to really hustle to get from that church up to the top of the hill (in almost complete darkness) so that he could come down it to give her that hug. In fact, the darkness and steepness of the hill in question would have kept most people from attempting such a trick.*

She adds: "My grandfather, one of the twins born after his father died, said that his mother would never go to church alone after that. In fact, to this day you will be hard-pressed to find one of us who would walk around the curve at the sulfur spring in the dark without someone with us."

In June 1962, Bedford, Trimble County, was visited by a what-do-you-call-it that was six feet tall, walked like a biped and was covered with hair. Witnesses claimed that its elongated arms reached its knees. A zoologist from Hanover College in Hanover, Indiana, examined its tracks and could not identify it.

Herrington Lake, Mercer County, is the alleged home of a fifteen-foot aquatic critter with a pig-like nose and a swinish, curly tail. The creature spent most of its time in the area between Chenault Bridge and Wells Landing and tended to surface early in the morning. Dr. Lawrence Sidney Thompson—scholar, author, one-time director of libraries at the University of Kentucky and for many years professor of classics at UK—bought a summer home at Herrington Lake in 1968 and saw the creature several times. In a 1972 interview with the *Courier-Journal*, Dr. Thompson suggested that a monster from a submerged cave got trapped in the lake when it was dammed by the Kentucky Utilities Company in 1924. The leading theory seems to be that the monster was actually an expatriated alligator, but at least no one claims that it escaped from a zoo or circus.

A Vegan's Worst Nightmare Comes True

At 11:00 a.m. on March 3, 1876, Mrs. Allen Crouch, a farmer's wife, was making soap in her yard at Mudlick Springs (also known as Olympian Springs) in Bath County, about seventeen miles east of Mount Sterling, Montgomery County. She noticed strange-looking particles floating down from the sky and coming from no apparent source. Disbelieving her eyes, she quickly called for her grandson and a boarding schoolmistress named Sadie Robinson. The boy also saw the odd scraps falling and Miss Robinson emerged from the house just in time to see the aftermath. The precipitation lasted only a few minutes and landed entirely on the Crouch farm. Accounts vary as to the size of the area that the falling flakes covered. The local paper, the *Bath County News*, said it was a piece of ground measuring roughly a hundred yards long and fifty yards wide, an estimate confirmed by Mr. Crouch's neighbor Harrison Gill; the *Courier-Journal* of March 9 gave the area as being one acre wide and two acres long; the next day the same paper made a claim of one hundred by two hundred yards. Whichever is correct, the major point is that the substance fell only in a small, localized area. The mysterious rain was not a widespread phenomenon.

When the shower ended, the witnesses went to see what had fallen. Much to their amazement and disgust, it appeared to be meat. The usual explanation for such bizarre showers is that the material was deposited by a not-too-distant tornado or thunderstorm, but by all accounts the meat rain fell on a sunny, pleasant day. One resident, Captain J.M. Bent, would recall that the weather was clear and that there was scarcely a cloud in the sky.

The substance resembled flakes of fresh beef or mutton ranging in size from one to four square inches. Though most of the pieces were dry, a few were of sufficient dampness to leave what appeared to be bloody streaks whenever they landed on something. The strips were half an inch to three-quarters of an inch in thickness. According to a *Courier-Journal* article published on March 11, "the flakes were from the size of a pea to that of a human finger, and rather thin." Mrs. Crouch later told a reporter: "The largest piece that I saw was as long as my hand, and about half an inch wide. It looked gristly, as if it had been torn from the throat of some animal." The strange scraps landed on the ground, on trees and on fences. The record does not state whether any enterprising children attempted to build snowmen (or rather meatmen) out of the flakes.

Hundreds of Bath Countians came to look at the "quivering flesh" that coated the ground like some obscene snowfall; the more superstitious onlookers were terrified and refused to touch the substance. Hogs, dogs and chickens had no such scruples and quickly ate most of the meat, if meat it was, to no ill effect. Mrs. Crouch's cat reportedly also devoured the repulsive manna. Only a few humans are known to have had the bravery to consume it. One man thought it tasted like mutton or venison; an elderly trapper named Benjamin Franklin Ellington swore that it was bear meat. A butcher from Mount Sterling named L.C. Frisby roasted the meat and found it edible but was unable to identify the animal from whence it came. He thought it resembled mutton but it had an unidentifiable smell and some watery fluid oozed from it. It was as tender as veal and Frisby noticed that it had "a fine, stringy fiber running through it, apparently in all directions."

Fortunately, some quick-thinking citizens collected and preserved a few specimens in alcohol. Harrison Gill, proprietor of Gill's Mudlick Sulfur Springs summer resort, sent a sample to Professor J. Lawrence Smith of Louisville, as did Captain J.M. Bent, the *Courier-Journal*'s Mount Sterling correspondent. When Professor Smith received Captain Bent's sample, he immediately remarked that it looked like animal tissue and said that he would give it a thorough scientific examination. We shall hear more of Smith's assessment later.

The meat rain was sensational news and not only in Kentucky. All over the nation, newspapers ran stories on the grotesque precipitation that had been visited upon Bath County. The periodical *Scientific American* carried a report in its March 25 issue and did a couple of follow-ups, according to paranormal researcher Charles Fort (I was not able to find the supplemental material he mentioned). The *New York Times* ran a page-one story on March 10 and the next day displayed its somewhat-creaky sense of humor in an editorial suggesting that the Crouch farm actually had been bombarded by meteorites (or should that be meat-eorites?) from some undiscovered asteroid belt consisting of meat instead of rocks. And where did this band of meat revolving around the sun come from? The *Times* suggested that it was the remains of the inhabitants of some exploded planet. In other words, the farm animals and the two brave Kentucky gentlemen had eaten alien carcasses.

The *New York Herald* referred to the strange occurrence in "the whisky state" and condescendingly imagined how puzzled the "quidnuncs" and "husking parties" in Kentucky must have been. The *Herald* patiently explained that showers of such critters as fish and frogs were fairly common and relied on the shopworn explanation that a cyclone could have carried away the substance elsewhere and dropped it on Bath County: "If the story…is true, the shower of quivering flesh was nothing more than a mass of the larvae of insects, which, having been caught up by a whirlwind and carried to an immense height, returned to earth again in the form of a shower of bruised and wriggling worms." The *Herald* apparently forgot that the "worms" dropped from a cloudless sky onto a relatively small patch of land and nowhere else. I checked the *Courier-Journal* of March

3, 4 and 5 and found no evidence that there had been any violent storms before the meat shower in the vicinity of Bath County or Kentucky in general. A witness named Dr. T.S. Bell recalled that the day was so calm that there was scarcely a breeze. One might also expect that if the "meat" were worm remains that at least a few of the hundreds of particles that fell would be clearly identifiable as such.

As the editorials in the *Times* and the *Herald* demonstrate, most papers took a lighthearted view of the meatfall. The *Chicago Times* insinuated that the precipitation consisted of "ordinary dog meat of the kind commonly used in making boarding-house sausages." The *Washington Chronicle* made the tongue-in-cheek suggestion that the story was a hoax intended to encourage immigration to Kentucky on the grounds that free lunches fell from the sky in that marvelous state. Like sentiments emanated from the *St. Louis Globe-Democrat*.

Newspaper editors weren't the only ones with theories. Scientists who had the chance to examine specimens of the meat weighed in with their learned opinions. The aforementioned Professor J. Lawrence Smith declared that the material was not meat, but dried "spawn" from some aquatic animal, with the frog being the most likely culprit. (It is not clear whether Smith was referring to eggs or already-hatched offspring.) The *Philadelphia Ledger* agreed with Smith and listed several examples of "miraculous" rainfalls through history, including falls of "blood," wheat, wool, frogs, fishes and many other things pleasant or unpleasant. The problem with Professor Smith's theory was that it would take an *awful* lot of frog spawn to cover so much ground. Also, as Captain Bent remarked, "[The theory] is very plausible, yet I never knew spawn to be at all red, and the flesh that fell contained a little of that color, though in the main white." Others who were skeptical of the skeptics' conclusions pointed out that the Bath County substance contained characteristics of animal flesh clearly visible to the naked eye, such as lean and fat, while frog spawn did not. Some questioned whether cats, dogs and other animals would even eat frog spawn.

And how did all of that alleged frog spawn get to one particular field in Bath County? By being carried aloft by a violent storm, said doubters. A Madison County resident wrote to the *Courier-Journal* on March 25:

> *During a tornado which passed over this place in February, a pond on the farm of Mr. W.R. Letcher, near Richmond, was completely drained of water, frogs, tadpoles and everything else, and there is no doubt but what the spawn of the frogs was taken up and went careering through the air until the force of the wind was spent, when it fell before Mrs. Crouch's astonished eyes.*

The *Courier-Journal* called the correspondent's theory "a plausible explanation." And it is certainly plausible unless you spend too much time wondering how any but the most violent yet sedentary of air currents could keep the material aloft several days over Kentucky, light though it might have been, until it finally was dropped in one narrow section of Bath County, merely a couple of counties away from Madison.

Another scientist, Dr. L.P. Yandell Sr., noted that another flesh shower had occurred near Lebanon, Tennessee, on August 17, 1841. He also said that while the frog spawn theory had its merits, he did not entirely believe it because some of the Bath County meat chunks had been bloody. Professor Smith countered that the meat from the shower could not have originated from grown mammals, for when he examined his samples he saw no blood corpuscles, nor "any animal tissue or structure, or muscular fiber, blood vessel, nervous tissue, etc." Smith described the material as being "simply unorganized, gelatinous matter"—in other words, the spawn of amphibians. He went on to state that a nearly identical "meat shower" had occurred once before in Kentucky, near Midway, Scott County, in spring 1818.

Sounds like an open-and-shut case, but in the *Scientific American* a Dr. Hamilton identified a specimen of the meat as being lung tissue, while other scientists' samples had indeed included cartilage or muscular fibers.

An alternative to the dried-spawn theory came from Leopold Brandeis, who claimed the substance was flesh-colored nostoc, a form of freshwater bluish-green algae that can form in gelatinous clumps. Brandeis theorized that the stuff had never fallen from the sky at all; it had lain unnoticed and dry on the ground. When it rained, said Brandeis, the nostoc swelled up and took on its mysterious meatlike appearance. Observers, untrained in the ways of science, simply assumed that it had fallen from the sky. However, Brandeis overlooked the fact that witnesses saw the material drifting down from the cloudless sky; also, for Brandeis's theory to be workable, it had to have rained —which it had not. And whatever it was that fell at Olympian Springs was pale, not bluish-green.

The most amazing theory of all came from Dr. A. Mead Edwards, president of the Newark Scientific Association, who hypothesized that the stuff had come from a flock of vomiting buzzards (which suggests that Dr. Edwards, unlike some of his peers, believed the material was authentic meat). The conjecture was not unique; in mid-March, the *Cincinnati Commercial* had published a letter signed "Old Farmer" advocating the same theory. "The fall of flesh… is nothing new," he wrote. "Some gorged buzzards have been unloading their stomachs in flying over after feeding on sheep killed by dogs." Old Farmer added, with what sounds to my ears like authority born of sorrowful firsthand experience, "I know about that."

The Barfing Buzzards Theory was delightful and imaginative, but like the other explanations, it had some problems. It would require a great number of vultures to so thoroughly coat a few acres with their lost lunches—and no witnesses saw this vast fleet of nauseous birds. The theory asks us to believe all the buzzards threw up at exactly the same time in the same location, even though there were no Michael Bolton albums in those days. It should be noted also that most of the meat, which was examined immediately after it fell, was dry rather than damp, as one would expect vulture vomit to be.

The meat rain became the subject of what we now call "urban legends," some of a very sinister nature. Rumor held that some of the pieces that had fluttered to earth had had toenails and fingernails. Some claimed that a man named Eli Wills had taken some of the flesh home to eat despite his family's strenuous objections. They were so terrified of the mystery meat that they seized the adventurous Mr. Wills, locked him in a room and buried his intended meal in the forest. It was said that a Mr. Armitage of Frenchburg was one of the first on the scene and when he touched a still-quivering piece of the fallen flesh, he got an electric shock that paralyzed his arm for a half hour. A story circulated in Mount Sterling that Mrs. Crouch had scattered the meat herself with the intention of scaring her husband into selling their farm, a charge that she vehemently denied before a reporter. (Mr. Crouch added that such tactics would not be necessary as he also wanted to sell the property.)

A couple of weeks after the incident, a *New York Herald* reporter named J.H. Almond visited the site of the meat shower and interviewed several witnesses including the Crouches and Frisby, the intrepid butcher. After Mrs. Crouch admitted that she found the event very unnerving and affirmed that the meat seemed to fall from overhead, the reporter asked where she thought the substance came from. She replied, "The Lord only knows…I have thought of it a heap, and it is the greatest mystery to me in the world." C.J. Craig saw the fleshy flakes just a couple hours after they fell and, while the pieces did not seem bloody, Craig noted that they did leave dark stains on whatever they touched, and "the smell was very peculiar, resembling that of fresh blood more than anything else." On the other hand, Reverend J.R. Nichols thought the meat did look bloody and, like many other witnesses, believed it resembled mutton. Storekeeper Joe Jordan saw some preserved samples a week after the incident; he found them dry, elastic, full of fibers and what looked like "brown mucous" and with an odor "offensive in the extreme, like a dead body." Nevertheless, he took a bite (who wouldn't?). He spat it out too quickly to perceive any taste.

Three weeks after the disgusting shower, a correspondent who signed his dispatch "J.H.A." (probably J.H. Almond) sent the *Courier-Journal* an update from Bath County. He found that the excitement had not yet died out; the post offices in the county and at Mount Sterling were still receiving so many letters from across the continent, asking for particulars about the meat shower, that postal workers found it impossible to answer them all. The journalist added that he had seen preserved samples of the substance and it looked a lot more like meat than batrachian spawn: "I have yet to see a single person who examined the article that fell, and also read Prof. Smith's published analysis, who has not said, in effect, that his judgment of it did not sustain the distinguished scientist in his estimate of its character." In other words, no one who saw the substance agreed with the professor's theory. By this time, very little of the grisly stuff was left, having mostly been consumed by livestock. "J.H.A." noted that Captain Bent still had a couple of specimens preserved in alcohol, one Vanarsdale of Frenchburg owned about twenty pieces and local resort owner Harrison Gill had several chunks in alcohol. The writer claimed that more scientific tests should be done on the existing samples, but it appears no one took him up on it. Dame Science had made up her mind and would tolerate no further questioning.

There the matter stands in an intolerable state of ambiguity. Perhaps someday a Bath Countian will rummage through a trunk full of forgotten souvenirs kept by his or her great-great-grandparents and will find a dusty old bottle containing a sample of the "meat" preserved in alcohol. Having read this invaluable book, he will recognize the nature of the found treasure. Then at last it may be analyzed and we will know what it truly was.

Light Beetle Showers This Morning, With a Chance of Knitting Needles This Afternoon

The Bath County meat shower aside, Kentucky has received its share of bizarre gifts from the sky. For some reason, an inordinate number of them occurred in Louisville. While the origin of the meat shower is debatable, the majority of outlandish showers almost certainly were the pranks of tornados and windstorms.

The strangest was a rain of knitting needles that fell on Harrodsburg, Mercer County, in 1856. (No source seems to mention the month in which it occurred.) Citizens arose after a stormy night to find an eight-acre lot on West Factory Street full of thousands of shiny new needles partially embedded slantwise in the ground and waving in the breeze "like a field of steel grass." Several prominent citizens—including Judge Thomas Cardwell, Fount Smedley, Isaac Pearson and Abe Stagg—swore in an affidavit that the strange rain had occurred. The *Harrodsburg Herald* reminisced in 1903:

Many people visited the scene the next day, coming from all parts of the county, and nearly everyone carried away a handful of the needles which in that day were a necessary adjunct in every household. Judge Cardwell, who was then a small boy, tells us that the morning after the shower his neighbor and chum, Dallas Chinn, came over to tell him of the wonderful thing that had happened, and they both hurried to the lot and got an armful of the needles, and afterward wore socks knitted with them.

Let it never be said that Kentuckians are not practical. As late as 1935, Neva Williams, assistant editor of the *Herald*, noted that she owned several of the steel needles that had been collected by her father.

It is likely that the needle rain was the work of a distant tornado, but the explanation is not entirely satisfactory. Why did all the needles land at the same angle, as though planted? Why did they fall in one narrow section of town and nowhere else? I searched many Kentucky newspapers dated throughout 1856 and found no reports of a tornado near Mercer County (or anywhere else) hitting a knitting needle factory. It is not certain that there even were any knitting needle factories in the state at the time. We must not rule out the possibility that the embedded needles were the fruit of a practical joker with money to burn and an exceedingly peculiar sense of humor.

On Sunday, August 24, 1879, the residents of Seventh and Eighth Streets in Louisville were favored with falling lizards and "waterdogs" (salamanders) along with rain of the mundane liquid sort. On September 6, 1880, Owingsville in Bath County was inflicted with a rain of lively water beetles. The bugs landed in puddles, in rain barrels, on rooftops, in gutters—but, as is often the case with this phenomenon, they fell in an almost absurdly localized area, on Main Street and a few blocks north. None fell south of Main Street. Sharpsburg and Mount Sterling also received some bugs from above that day, but those towns were not blessed as copiously as Owingsville, the citizens of which had not yet quite recovered froFm the mystery of the meat shower. The next day, Louisville and Clark County, Indiana, got a light sprinkling of the same species of beetle. A number of the bugs were placed in a jar of water and put on display at Dr. Graham's Museum. On July 20, 1882, Louisville received yet another rain of bugs by the thousands, an event that reminded many of the plague God wrought upon the pharaoh of Egypt. They covered the city's electric lights and citizens were disgusted by the fumes that emanated from the burning insects when the critters ventured too close to power sources. The bugs were described as having "long, lank bodies, immense sail-like wings and preternaturally wise-looking little beads of eyes."

A veritable menagerie rained on Louisville on the night of April 15, 1885. The old standby explanation—that a storm lifted the wee beasties from some other location, carried them aloft for a while, then dumped them—is likely true in this case as well, but the occurrence is not without mystery. The denizens of Market Street first saw what appeared to be white meteors streaking by in the heavens. Then came a downpour of an estimated five thousand birds "of all sizes and shades," though mostly white and resembling the canary. Other specimens of indignant fowl appeared to be quail, martins and bluebirds. This was followed by a shower of grasshoppers and earthworms. The grand finale was a heavy rain—of water. "[M]arvelous as this account may read, it is nevertheless true, and can be substantiated by a score of reputable men and women," said the *Courier-Journal* the next day. On June 27, 1889, Louisville was once again the location of a capricious act of nature. This time it was a shower of frogs that fell on an area of four blocks between Twenty-First and Bank Streets. It happened again on July 19, 1894, but only on Sixteenth Street. Then, on April 23, 1900, workers at the Louisville reservoir were soaked by falling rain and live fish of varying sizes and species. Enough fish fell to provide the laborers with a "heaven-sent" lunch.

In 1892, Jack Ritchey's farm, five miles from Hawesville on the Patesville pike, received a shower of small green plums not native to the area during a spell of wet, stormy weather. The plums fell on an area of Ritchey's farm "not larger than a room," and nowhere else in the vicinity. It was the wonder of Hancock County for a while but was largely forgotten—until 1897, when, during a spate of stormy weather, more of the same plums fell from the sky on exactly the same spot. The phenomenon happened at least twice more: in January 1898 and in March 1899. Then it appears to have ceased, though Hawesville received a rain of thousands of green worms on June 8, 1902.

Readers of my book *Murder in Old Kentucky* will remember the tale of Lucretia Mundy, a Woodford County widow who went on trial several times on a charge of having poisoned her husband in 1883. She at last was acquitted in February 1888. As if she didn't have enough trouble, in July 1886 her neighborhood, Mundy's Landing, was subjected to rains of stones falling from the sky—not once, but several times. Most of the incidents took place at or close to the accused woman's mansion. The first precipitation came on July 19, when persons picking blackberries not far from Mrs. Mundy's house were pelted by small rocks falling from above. The next day, a Mrs. Davis (probably Lucretia's daughter) was severely injured by a rock falling on her arm and Miss Annie Mundy was hit on the head. Eva Mundy was struck by a falling rock the day after that and a man named Henry was hit so hard by a stone that he nearly fell off a cliff. Over the course of one weekend, several people were injured, a couple severely, by a rain of rocks. Houses were also pounded by the missiles. One day, Lucretia Mundy herself was rained upon as she walked in her garden. She high-tailed it back into the house, but not before at least one rock inflicted a serious injury. Her roof sustained some damage. Allegedly, she was so alarmed that she fled the neighborhood. A few days later, laborers working on the grounds were so heavily clobbered by stones from the heavens that they fled for their lives.

Witnesses claimed that the rocks descended vertically, as though falling from far above, not horizontally or at an angle, as one would expect if they were simply being tossed by hiding pranksters. In any case, the Mundy residence

was located in a wide-open space far from the cliffs where hypothetical rock-tossers could hide. Some of the missiles were collected and taken to Daughters College in Harrodsburg for scientific analysis, but the papers appear not to have reported the results. Adding to the mystery, the stones that fell were of a color different from the local rocks. Many citizens considered the unorthodox showers a judgment from God on Lucretia Mundy, who some felt appeared to be getting away with murder. Why so many innocent people also should be wounded by the falling rocks, they did not seem to ponder.

Even stranger was the case of twelve-year-old Onie York (daughter of Jim B. York), who was showered with rocks on a regular basis yet somehow seemed to be conjuring them up herself. The family lived about four miles from Benton, Marshall County. "It is claimed that wherever she goes, rocks fall in great numbers continually," reported the *Paducah Leader* circa September 1899. "They seem to start about two feet above her head, but the source of the rocks can not be seen. They are not large, but about the size of a pebble [to] the dimensions of a hen egg." Strangely, the rocks seemed to fall in slow motion.

Skeptical persons locked Onie up in a rockless room. "When placed in the room no rocks were on her person," assures the reporter. (One wonders, however, how closely they were willing to search a little girl's clothes.) When the door was opened later, the floor was literally covered with rocks. Said the *Leader* reporter: "Hundreds of people have visited the girl and tell the same story and say it is the most remarkable event in Marshall County's history. The girl's father, not being a man of wealth, has offered a fine span of mules if anyone will solve the mystery," and a wealthy citizen named Bud Hunt offered a $100 reward to anyone who could find the source of the rocks. The account adds that "Polk Rose, another highly respected citizen of that county, vouches for the veracity of the case, and says the rocks are still falling." Where and when the phenomenon came to an end, and whether wee Onie was playing a good practical joke on the grown-ups, no one seems to know.

They Might Be Giants

In his book *Weird America*, author Jim Brandon mentions several towns in the United States where the skeletal remains of giants have been found: Lompoc Rancho, California; Brewersville and Walkerton, Indiana; Chatfield and Clearwater, Minnesota; several towns in Wisconsin, including Dresbach; Lovelock, Nevada; and Tioga Point, Pennsylvania, where a mound contained no fewer than sixty-eight skeletons averaging seven feet in length. On many occasions, the Bluegrass State has yielded surrealistically elongated skeletons.

For example, a burial mound on the farm of Eden Burrowes near Franklin, Simpson County, was excavated in May 1841. Several skeletons were found at a depth of twelve feet. Most of them were of ordinary appearance but one skeleton, found lying between two logs and covered with a wooden slab, was that of a human so tall that the leg bones were about six inches longer than average. The lower jawbone could fit completely over the jaw of an ordinary man. The giant had been buried wearing a necklace consisting of 1 silver bead and 120 copper beads.

In late July or early August 1850, at Rolling Fork, Hardin County, twelve miles from Elizabethtown, John Harned found a human thighbone six times the number of cubic inches as that of an average man. Harned also found a collarbone of the same proportions. "That it is a human bone there can be no doubt," said the *Elizabethtown Register*. It was calculated that the bones' original possessor must have been twelve or thirteen feet tall.

The *Cincinnati Chronicle* reported circa February 1870 that a surveyor had discovered giant human footprints in limestone rock near Grayson Springs, Grayson County. He also found imbedded tracks of horses, mules and colts.

Harrison Whaley, a farmer of Moorefield, Nicholas County, owned a tract of woods in the early 1870s that teemed with skeletons and burial mounds. One particular mound yielded clay utensils, arrowheads, pipes and "skulls and bones, which, from their size, must have belonged to a race of beings far more gigantic than the race which now inhabits the earth," in the words of the *Carlisle Mercury*.

The 1878 edition of Collins's *History of Kentucky* notes that coal prospectors a mile from Rockport, Ohio County, found a complete giant human skeleton buried six feet below the sod "in early 1872." The lower jawbone was so large that it covered most of the face of a man of average size. The thighbone was forty-two inches long; the forearm, twenty-two inches. When alive, the human would have been over ten feet tall. Through the magic of backbreaking research,

I have determined that the giant was found in April 1872 on a farm belonging to Tuck Austin.

Robert Render Sr. discovered another dead giant in Ohio County, near Green River. According to historian Harrison D. Taylor, Render was over six feet tall; the skeleton was that of a man one-third larger than Render, making its original owner at least eight feet tall in life. Taylor wrote in 1926, "It is now a subject of regret that this grave had not been thoroughly examined by scientific men, and a full skeleton procured of this semi-giant race."

The *Trigg County Democrat* reported in November 1877:

> *A laborer engaged…in digging holes in a lot near the famous mound in Canton, for the purpose of building a post and railing fence for Dr. Lackey, unearthed a number of skeletons. The skull and jawbone of one of them evidently belonged to a race of giants. The lower jaw found fitted easily over the chin and lower extremity of the face of Mr. Bailey Tompkins, a well known citizen of the place, whose facial developments at these points are large and covered with a heavy beard. On the breast of the skeleton was found a stone spearhead, about eighteen inches in length, showing that the remains belonged at least to some great chief of the aborigines, a "head and shoulders taller" than any of the tribes known to exist on the continent.*

The citizens of Caneyville, Grayson County, were considerably excited in January 1885, when someone discovered a burial ground in the forks of Caney Creek, a mile and a half from town. The excitement turned to wonder when excavators turned up fire coals, clay pottery and a number of skeletons "of very large stature" buried between large flat rocks rather than in coffins. An observer wrote: "Who these people were and to what race they belonged is, and perhaps will ever remain, a mystery."

One of the wonders of Madison County in the late nineteenth century was a three-acre prehistoric cemetery located on two adjoining farms, one belonging to Caldwell Campbell and the other to brothers Samuel and Walker Mason. The burial site, located eight miles southwest of Richmond, contained the bones of a gigantic race. When the remains were compared to the anatomy of one John Campbell, himself unusually tall at six feet four inches, it became evident that the skeletons were those of people between seven and eight feet tall. The farm of G.B. Turley, near Richmond, bore another seven-foot skeleton in late September 1891. This one had been buried under a large flat rock with seven smaller corpses.

In July 1894, Colonel Bennett Young of the Filson Club, later the author of *Prehistoric Men of Kentucky* (1910), explored a large burial mound on the property of John Moberly two miles south of Waco, Madison County. As on the Turley farm, the mound housed the remains of six persons of average size and "a person of tremendous stature," in Young's words, approximately one-third larger than his fellow skeletons, making him at least seven feet tall in life. The mound also yielded quantities of charcoal, white clay, copper beads,

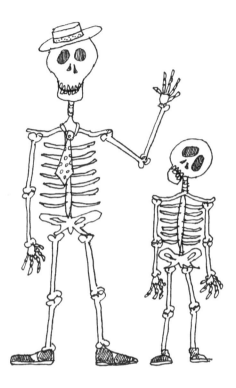

arrowheads, six spearheads (one black, one yellow, four blue), stone fleshers, pieces of mica, a pipe, a whetstone and other exotic relics of the past. This was undoubtedly the best-documented find of a giant skeleton in Kentucky. Colonel Young wrote two articles about it for the *Courier-Journal*, one of which included a drawing of the giant's jawbone, which came complete with perfect pearly white teeth. Young submitted the bones to doctors, who concurred that he had indeed unearthed the remains of a giant human.

Using the pen name "John Avroe Steele," Judge Rollin T. Hurt recalled in his *History of Adair County* that several ancient burial mounds were located near the Moffett McGill house. "A number of skeletons were exhumed there," he wrote, "one of which was that of a man, who in life was above seven feet in height, and in the same grave were the skeletons of a small human being and a dog." According to Judge Hurt, children and the superstitious regarded the place with awe: "The writer very well remembers that when a child and residing upon an adjoining farm, he has crept with much dread to the top of the Cedar Cliff, and from there peered through the overhanging bushes and vines at the McGill house and the locality about it, and then cautiously and silently crept away."

In October 1893, Robert Carter of Middlesboro and a friend went cave exploring near Tampico, Taylor County (now Coburg, Adair County). They found several skeletons, one of which was that of a man at least eight feet tall. Its head, shoulders, arms and thighbones were intact, but some bones had petrified and become "hard as flint."

In late 1893 or early 1894, some men excavated a mound on the Kentucky River bank below Carrollton, Carroll County. Ten feet down, they found three skeletons "of gigantic size," their arms and legs covered with beads that appeared to be made of some animal's teeth.

One fine day in autumn 1896, John Winter of Elkwell Creek, Bell County, was digging a cellar in his home when his spade uncovered a canoe-shaped coffin containing an eight-foot mummy swaddled in a winding sheet made of animal skins. The mummy was equipped with a stone hatchet, a shield made of skin, cooking utensils and a hollow stone that presumably once contained a meal. Unfortunately for posterity, the mummy and his shield crumbled into dust shortly after being exposed to air.

The year 1897 was congested with giant skeletons. A Cynthiana paper reported in April that John Hill unearthed a seven-foot-plus skeleton while digging a foundation for a milk house. As in the Bell County case described above, the skeleton had been buried with weapons and trinkets and disintegrated into ashes after its discovery. In the same month, an Indian mound was opened on the farm of William Thresher, near Lewisport, Hancock County. County Jailer William Brown, who was present, reported that the mound contained six skeletons of ordinary size and one that was at least nine feet long with a skull double the size of an average man's. It was placed on exhibition, but its present whereabouts are unknown. In late April or early May, William Gibson of Bennett's Fork, Bell County, unearthed a stone coffin while plowing. Inside were "human bones of enormous size."

Allen County has long been noted for its Indian burial mounds, some of which tenanted the remains of giants. A writer in 1899 noted that some years before, Dr. J.B. Walker of Scottsville had measured a thighbone retrieved from one of the sites and had determined that its possessor must have been ten feet tall. In the summer of 1925, it was reported that Allen County mounds still yielded "thigh bones [that] measured from eight to ten inches longer than the race of men now inhabiting the country."

In 1900, Charles Portwood of Locust Grove, Boone County, was reported to have found a number of Indian burial mounds on the cliffs overlooking Gunpowder Creek. These he excavated and found "several large skeletons," at least one of which was over seven feet in height.

An occurrence on or around July 15, 1901, demonstrated that it wasn't just country folk who found the remains of giants. Workmen extending Burnett Avenue in Louisville uncovered a seven-foot skeleton under an oak tree at the corner of Shelby and Burnett. It had been buried in a sitting position and was accompanied by a two-pound tomahawk. Coroner McCullough sagely decided that an inquest would be pointless. Legend held that an Indian brave named Masatonah, seven feet two inches in size, had been shot by two Louisville pioneers around 1786. The best anyone could figure was that Masatonah's remains had been found. The bones were wired together at the morgue and, at last report, they were to be "displayed in a suitable place" for the public.

Almost a decade later, Louisville yielded more giants in the earth. At the end of March 1910, workers constructing the new Windsor Place subdivision near Von Borries Avenue and Bardstown Road dug up "three skeletons of enormous size." Allegedly hundreds of citizens, including several doctors, visited the site and saw the remains. Coroner Ellis Duncan decided that two skeletons were male and one was female. Dr. Duncan declared that he would investigate the matter and that was the last heard of it.

In mid-November 1911, a farmer named Hugh Yates reportedly unearthed a twelve-footer in a cave at the foot of a cliff on his farm at Vine Grove, Hardin County. He also found many other skeletons "of gigantic proportions" and relics including "curiously wrought jewels," ornaments, cooking vessels and strangely designed musical instruments. The news inspired a slightly flippant editorial in the December 28 *Louisville Courier-Journal*, which remarked: "Such places of sepulchre are not uncommon in Kentucky and they are supposed to date back a matter of 2,000 years. It is evident that 'there were giants in those days,' but the people now on earth do not know or care much about them."

To the sorrow of future anthropologists, nothing of the remains or relics from these archaeological finds seems to have been preserved. Several discomfiting questions arise if we assume that not all of the above accounts are journalistic hoaxes and that our ancestors were bright enough to distinguish between human and dinosaur bones. Where did these giants come from? Were they Indians, Vikings or other pre-Columbian explorers from Europe? Or were they members of a long-extinct race of humans? Whatever they were, it appears that there were plenty of them.

The Lexington Catacombs

It has been rumored for decades that the city of Lexington was constructed atop a complex system of catacombs built by the lost Indian race called the Mound Builders. The story attained respectability when historian George Washington Ranck mentioned it in his 1872 book *History of Lexington, Ky*. (Harrodsburg is a Kentucky city that definitely sits atop an enormous cave, but that is another story.)

According to Ranck, the Fayette County catacombs were discovered in 1776, three years before Lexington was settled, by "some venturesome hunters, most probably from Boonesborough" in Madison County—though it must be said that twenty-odd miles is a long way to go to bag a deer. The hunters saw stones "of peculiar workmanship" on the site of what later would become Lexington. When they removed the rocks, the hunters found a concealed ancient catacomb in stone fifteen feet below the surface of the earth.

The explorers climbed into the hole and found that the tunnel expanded as they progressed. Soon they were walking comfortably through a stone hallway four feet wide and seven feet high. The floor of the tunnel became a ramp that ran downward a few hundred feet and ended in an enormous chamber three hundred feet long, one hundred feet wide, eighteen feet high and full of niches into which were crammed a number of mummies in a "perfect state of preservation."

A few years passed before the catacombs could be thoroughly explored, for until 1782 the land was the site of many wars between the settlers and the Indians. According to Ranck, "the catacomb was despoiled [during the battles] and its ancient mummies…were well nigh swept out of existence." Some remained intact, however, and allegedly the tunnel and mummy room were minor tourist attractions for a few years. The Irish travel writer Thomas Ashe is supposed to have seen them in 1806. The story goes that the entrance to the tunnel was eventually lost and forgotten due to urban expansion.

Unlike so many wild legends from the past, the story of the Lexington catacombs is plausible. Other amazing and bizarre constructions were found in the vicinity long ago, though whether they were built by Indians or explorers from elsewhere is an unsettled matter. The historian John Filson reported that ancient stone tombs of pyramidal shape were at Lexington as late as 1784 and remarked, "They are built in a way totally different from that of the Indians." That the Indians (or somebody) constructed elaborate monuments, fortifications and burial mounds around Lexington is well documented by Ranck.

Two major authorities in the field, W.D. Funkhouser and W.S. Webb, dismissed the story of the chamber full of mummies but acknowledged that Lexington is built atop limestone caves. However, it stands to reason that if the mysterious architects who built the surface structures had found a system of limestone caverns, they could have improved them and used them. Perhaps someday Lexington construction workers will drill through some antiquated piece of pavement and get the surprise of their lives.

Tales From the Graveyard

The Music Teacher's Last Request

Jessie E. Clinton was a black music teacher who lived in turn-of-the-century Kentucky. In August 1896, she moved from Louisville to Somerset, Pulaski County. Her specialty was the piano, an instrument at which she excelled. Tragically, her teaching career was cut short when she contracted tuberculosis around September 1896 and had to move into her mother's home at 632 Laurel Street, Louisville. During her illness, she practiced daily on the piano that had been her prized possession for a decade. When at last she became too weak to play, visiting neighbors would cheer her up by playing it for her. When Miss Clinton died on February 6, 1897, her mother carried out her strange last request: at the wake, her body was laid out for viewing not in a coffin, but atop her piano.

Macabre Practical Jokes

How seriously did some people believe in ghosts back in the good old days? Seriously enough to become physically stricken if they thought they saw one, as the following story of a prank gone wrong illustrates.

Joseph Huangs, a Louisville barkeeper, had been married only five months. On the night of January 1, 1897, Mrs. Huangs went upstairs to their quarters over the saloon while her husband stayed downstairs, balancing the day's accounts. He had been at work only a few minutes when he heard her scream. Seconds later, she came stumbling back downstairs. "Great heavens!" she said. "There is a strange woman upstairs. Oh, she is so pale and frightful looking." When she had recovered sufficiently from her fright, Mrs. Huangs said the woman was tall, wore ordinary clothes and looked "very unnatural," with dead, immobile features. Mr. Huangs went upstairs to investigate and there in the dark he found what had frightened his wife.

Some practical joker had stuffed a calico dress and put a "false face" where the head should be. He had also put a hood on the figure, placed shoes under the dress, and given it gloves in lieu of hands. As a finishing touch, he pinned a note reading "A Happy New Year" to one of its arms. Mrs. Huangs had been so terrified by the figure that her health went into immediate decline. Mr. Huangs told the press that he thought he knew the culprit's identity and said that if his suspicions proved correct, he would take drastic measures to improve the man's sense of humor. The papers

did not report further developments, but let's hope Mr. Huangs taught the prankster a harsh life lesson.

The Moellman family, also of Louisville, was subjected to an even more malevolent death-oriented prank. Seventeen-year-old Benjamin had been afflicted with a heart condition for about four years. As the year 1905 drew to a close, he was confined to his deathbed. On Christmas Eve, an anonymous black package addressed to the young man arrived at the family's East Madison Street residence. It contained a funeral shroud along with a card wishing Benjamin "A Merry Christmas and a Happy New Year." Fortunately, the boy's father, grocer August Moellman, opened the package. Rather than inform the family about the contents of the disturbing "gift," he threw the package and the cheery card into the furnace. Benjamin Moellman, who had no known enemies, died thirteen hours after the shroud's arrival.

They Got Lost

When a cave in southern Muhlenberg County was explored in November 1872, spelunkers found an entire preserved family: a man holding a child of about ten and a woman holding an infant. As if that were not sufficiently outlandish, the man and woman were dressed in clothes like those worn by ancient Romans. The story was likely a journalistic hoax, but no proof one way or the other has been forthcoming.

A Libel in Stone

In 1885, John Harvey, a teenager in Smith's Grove, Warren County, got into a scrap with a larger classmate named Brooks LaRue Shobe, age sixteen. When the dust settled, Harvey had stabbed Shobe to death. During the first trial, the jury was deadlocked; during the second, Harvey was acquitted. There the matter rested until 1897, when Harvey found that Shobe's wealthy relatives had recently put up a new tombstone at the grave bearing the epitaph "He Fell by Assassin's Hands," implying that Harvey had murdered Shobe intentionally and with malice aforethought. In February 1898, Harvey brought a libel suit against his victim's father, E.A. Shobe, and grandfather, Dr. T.B. LaRue, claiming $20,000 in damages. When the case went before the Warren Circuit Court, Harvey won. Shobe and LaRue were ordered to pay Harvey's court costs and to remove the offending words from the gravestone.

Citizen Cane

George Yates, a member of the famous First Kentucky Confederate Brigade (the "Orphan Brigade"), was killed at the Battle of Chickamauga in September 1863 and buried on the battlefield. Twenty-three years later, Jake Sandusky, a fellow soldier, was present when Yates's remains were exhumed. Sandusky found to his surprise that a small hickory tree had sprouted through Yates, its roots intertwined with his bones. Sandusky turned the hickory tree into a walking cane with a silver knob on top, engraved with a drawing of two crossed Confederate flags and the word "Chickamauga." The rest of Yates's remains were buried in Frankfort. Near the turn of the century, Sandusky, then living in Wilmore, Jessamine County, sent the cane to Yates's brother, Judge J.J. Yates of Scott County, at the judge's request. The cane, made from a tree that had been nourished by a soldier's body, became a prized family heirloom.

Midnight Funeral

R.H. Ware, an undertaker of Brooksville, Bracken County, witnessed so much "insincerity and vain display" at funerals throughout his career that he expressed a final wish to be buried at midnight so his funeral would be "as quiet as possible." He died on Friday, September 2, 1898, and according to his wishes was buried at the witching hour on Sunday night as a female mourner warbled "Nearer My God to Thee." The *Maysville Bulletin* remarked, "The weird scene will hardly ever be forgotten by any who witnessed it."

The Convict's Grave

At the dawn of the twentieth century, visitors to the cemetery at Eddyville, Lyon County, had their curiosity provoked by a solitary grave located in a distant corner of the graveyard, just outside the fence and far from all the other plots. It was the final resting place of a convict who had died of consumption in Eddyville Prison circa 1896, at the age of thirty-seven. His father, who lived in the other end of the state, sent hard-earned money to have his son buried in a place of honor in the local cemetery rather than in the prison cemetery. However, law-abiding citizens objected to having a criminal buried near their own dearly departed. As a compromise, the convict was buried just beyond the bounds of the cemetery. The convict's father later paid to have a tombstone erected and a little fence built around the grave. I have been unable to find out whether the convict is still isolated from his neighbors or whether the land around his grave has been annexed due to space considerations.

Skeletal Surprises

A surprise and a mystery awaited the workers who were removing the old stairs leading into the office of the clerk of the court of appeals in Frankfort in late August 1889. Under one stair, they found a decayed box containing the bones of a human child estimated to have been two or three years old at the time of its death. No one knew how the pathetic remains came to be there, but they must have been in the secret hiding place since 1832, the year the building was constructed.

On March 21, 1899, in Murray, Calloway County, Samuel Dent was cutting up a large tree he had felled near the Marshall County border when he found a human skeleton entombed within a hollow cyst in the tree. The skeleton's presence was a mystery, but one theory seemed better than most: in 1869 or 1870, a group of raccoon hunters had been hunting in the area when one of their party, a man named Bardman, disappeared without a trace. It was deemed likely that all those years ago he had climbed up the tree to get his prey when he slipped and fell into a hollow place and met a horrible death by suffocation or starvation.

The Rockcastle County Circuit Clerk's office once housed the skeleton of James S. Miller, who was murdered in Pulaski County in 1864. His bones were used as evidence during the trial of his killers and then buried in a cave. Around 1877, the remains were disinterred and brought to Mount Vernon as a curiosity. Somehow, they ended up in a box in the clerk's office and may be there yet.

In September 1903, gravediggers accommodating the remains of Mr. Edward Bryan in the Hickory Ridge Cemetery near Aberdeen, Butler County, made an intriguing discovery when they reached a depth of five feet. They found what appeared to be an old-fashioned hog trough made out of a hollow log, with a door on top of it. When they removed the door, they beheld a skeleton which had suffered the indignity of having its legs chopped off. A similar case occurred in May 1905: while engaged in digging the grave of Mrs. Anna Major Fairbourn in Frankfort Cemetery, workers found a strangely persecuted skull. Its frontal bones had been crushed and someone had taken the trouble to drive two long nails into its left side. Cemetery officials could find no record of anyone ever having been buried on that spot. Medical examiners determined that the skull had been buried for about fifty years and its original owner had been a young male.

Thomas Dunn of Danville got a delightful surprise in January 1903, when he unearthed the skeleton of some creature that had a head like a monkey. The rest of its body seemed to be half-monkey and half-fish. The description is a little too close to that of P.T. Barnum's "Fiji Mermaid" hoax for comfort.

History remembers Junius Brutus Booth not only as the father of John Wilkes, but also as one of the greatest actors of the nineteenth century. His performances in the role of Hamlet were particularly legendary and it was well known that he used a genuine human skull as a prop during the famous graveyard speech: "Alas, poor Yorick! I knew him, Horatio…" What was *not* well known was that he obtained the skull in Kentucky. In the early 1840s, Booth had befriended a western scoundrel whose name unfortunately has been lost to the ages. Years passed and Booth forgot about his former friend. One morning as he was staying in a Louisville hotel, a messenger delivered a woven basket containing the head of the scoundrel, who had willed it to Booth in hopes that he would use it when playing Hamlet. After he got over his initial shock, the eccentric Booth was happy to comply with the bequest. The skull was used onstage for many years afterward by his son Edwin, who kept it on a bracket in his apartment at the Players, a social club in New York City.

Funereal Fisticuffs

When Mary Wethers died in Louisville in spring 1899, her funeral was held at home, as was the custom of the time. At her wake, a full-scale war erupted among her family members. She had been insured and since her sister Alice had paid most of the premiums on the policy, she felt that she was entitled to the insurance money. On the day of the funeral, April 3, the father of the deceased, Edward Wethers, called in an undertaker to give Mary a proper burial. But sister Alice demanded a cheaper service and brother Silas objected to the father's choice of an undertaker. Simmering hostilities turned into an argument and the argument turned into a battle royale. The funeral director was forced to run for his life as the Wethers family flung every object that was not nailed down at each other, including but not limited to buckets full of ashes, kegs and furniture. At one point, Silas Wethers drew a pistol on his father. The "services" came to an end when Mary's remains were forcibly removed from the household. Alice defiantly sat on the coffin as the officials carried it downstairs.

Three Graves, One Body

Young Martin Railey died of consumption in the winter of 1901. Before he passed into the Great Beyond, Railey requested that he be buried beside his sister in a cemetery near Gatewood, Daviess County. His Gatewood neighbors dug a grave for him and gathered for a funeral, only to find that because of the foul weather, he had been more conveniently buried in the Nicholas Cemetery in Hancock County. The hundred or so mourners filled in the hole and left in disappointment. Railey's father felt remorseful about having failed to fulfill his son's dying wish and he had the remains exhumed eight days after the interment. A third grave was dug in Daviess County and there Martin Railey stays.

Taking Another Direction

It is a tradition since time immemorial to bury the dead facing east. Not so, however, in the case of Henry M. Richie, a Confederate veteran who lived near Blue Rock Springs, Nicholas County. Just before he died on October 9, 1902, he requested that his body be wrapped in his tattered old army blanket and buried facing south.

Three Long-Delayed Burials

The infant son of Dr. and Mrs. Miles White died in Owensboro on September 15, 1893, but due to protracted legal problems, the embalmed body remained in the possession of undertaker Robert Tennelly. It was at last buried in Elmwood Cemetery in June 1904. By then, the parents had moved to parts unknown and no witnesses were at the burial except the son of Robert Tennelly, a newspaper reporter and a gravedigger who bore the evocative nickname "Ant."

Charles "Speedy" Atkins of Paducah, McCracken County, is a legendary character. Around May 28, 1928, Atkins—a fiftysomething black vagrant—fell under the influence and drowned in the Ohio River. His body was taken to the A.Z. Hamock Funeral Home, where the proprietor tested his homemade secret formula embalming fluid on Atkins's corpse. The stuff worked so well that Atkins's body became more or less mummified. Since Atkins had no next of kin, Hamock kept the well-dressed body on display in his funeral home for decades—never for profit, let it be said. When Hamock died in 1949, his widow Velma took over the business. Speedy's remains proved quite a draw and he appeared on national television three times. He was at last buried in Paducah's Maplelawn Cemetery on August 5, 1994.

Edmonson County's famous, ill-fated cave explorer Floyd Collins is Speedy's chief rival for the record for the most time a Kentuckian has spent above ground postmortem. Many Americans are familiar with the grim cautionary tale that is inextricably connected to Floyd's demise. At the end of January 1925, Collins went exploring the small Sand Cave alone. As he inched his way through a narrow, dark crawlspace, a rock became dislodged and pinned his left leg. Unable to move forward or backward, Collins was trapped. Although well-wishers were able to get close enough to talk to Collins and keep him supplied with food and blankets, the passageway was too narrow to allow them to remove the rock on his leg. Within days, the frantic rescue efforts were the talk of the world. As various methods were attempted to reach Collins, a carnival-like atmosphere prevailed on the surface outside the cave, complete with lines of automobiles belching forth tourists and hawkers of souvenirs and snack foods. Millions of newspaper readers and radio listeners waited breathlessly each day to find out whether Collins had been saved or had died. The answer came on February 16, when would-be rescuers finally completed digging a shaft and lateral tunnel. Collins had died a slow, miserable, lonely death due to exposure.

His body remained in Sand Cave until April 23, when his family retrieved the corpse and gave it a proper burial. In 1927, Dr. Harry Thomas, an entrepreneur with a taste for the macabre, bought nearby Crystal Cave—a cave Collins himself had discovered in 1917—from the dead man's father; to make the cave even more of a tourist attraction, Thomas exhumed Collins's body via legally shady means and exhibited it in a glass-covered casket. For decades, any tourist who had a mind to do so could open the casket and gaze at the preserved countenance of "the Greatest Cave Explorer Ever Known," as his tombstone called him. Collins's body went on an adventure in March 1929, when someone broke into the cave and stole the corpse. It was later found on a riverbank not far from the cave, wrapped in a sack and with the left leg—the one that had been pinned down by the rock—mysteriously missing. The corpse was returned to the casket, but the missing leg was never found. The coffin was finally discreetly covered in 1948, though generously tipping tourists were still allowed to peek at Collins's body to their hearts' content. In 1961, the National Park Service bought Crystal Cave and closed it to the public—but the casket containing the remains stayed put, unvisited and alone in the stygian blackness of the abandoned cave.

At last, Collins's descendants won the legal right to inter his corpse. He was removed from Crystal Cave and buried in the Mammoth Cave Baptist Church Cemetery on March 24, 1989—sixty-four years after his death.

Death Warnings

Here are a couple of uncanny stories about Louisvillians whose deaths were predicted by others. A native named Zang moved to Little Rock, Arkansas, around February 1880. On April 5, as Zang stood at the cigar stand in the Capital Hotel, he was approached by a complete stranger, a reverend named McDonald. The preacher said to Zang: "Are you hungry? Does your soul thirst for anything?" He then reached out, placed his hand over Zang's heart, and said: "You have a very short time to live. If you have any arrangements to make in this world, make them." McDonald walked away without another word. Zang was troubled enough to express a determination to make sure his insurance was in order. Then he checked into the Benevolent Hospital. Later that night, Zang got out of bed and collapsed, dying soon afterward. An autopsy showed that he had been in the final stages of pleuropneumonia; his lungs were all but gone.

Mrs. Peterman, a medium who lived on Shelby Street, gave the following prognostication to Dr. Alfred Lemberger, a resident of the Germantown neighborhood, in late September 1901: "Within nine days [your] fine mare will die; the colt that you value will die; your last hunting dog will disappear, and then you will die." The doctor was untroubled and later that day told the details to his companions as they played cards. "Boys," he said, "You can play cards on my coffin in a couple of weeks if the prophecy a woman made today comes true."

"Within nine days your fine mare will die…"

Soon after Lemberger made his flippant remarks at the card game, his mare did die of colic; the countdown had begun.

"The colt that you value will die…"

Three days after the mare's demise, the colt died of pleurisy. "I don't see how the colt got pleurisy in that stable," the veterinarian remarked.

"Your last hunting dog will disappear…"

The morning after the colt's death, Dr. Lemberger's "last good hunting dog" disappeared, and two puppies died the same day.

"…and then you will die."

By this point, the doctor was no longer laughing. He went fishing one day, but left melancholy instructions as to what should be done in case he did not return. He only went out at night in the company of others. On the evening of the ninth day, he went to play his weekly game of cards with his friends. He was in good spirits again, probably thinking he had defeated the prediction. There was much morbid joking at the doctor's expense. The merriment lasted until the doctor said, "I bid two." Just then, as he sat in his chair, he saw the Death Angel's smiling, effulgent countenance. Dr. Lemberger was buried in Cave Hill Cemetery on October 6. A few weeks later, the *Courier-Journal* noted that since predicting the physician's death, "Mrs. Peterman has received an average of twenty-five letters a day from people all over the country asking for her aid in various ways." There is no record that she met again with such success.

No Dogs Allowed

James Crews of Rockcastle County was a tavern keeper and operator of the Crews Ferry on the Rockcastle River. He loved hunting and was also wealthy and eccentric. These traits mingled after he was murdered in 1862 about the age of fifty-five. He was buried in a tomb laboriously chiseled in a solid sandstone rock on top of a mountain about six miles from Livingston. He had requested that his body be placed there "so that his hounds could not run over him." To make matters stranger, it was erroneously rumored that he had been buried with money and his remote grave was vandalized a number of times by treasure seekers. At one point, they stole his body, presumably in a spirit of revenge, and took his skull to Dayton, Ohio, for purposes undivulged. In 1975, local historian John Lair wrote that he visited Crews's empty sepulcher and found "the stone marker bearing Crews's name and burial date…still lying beside the open grave in undamaged condition."

Langford's Sarcophagus

Readers of my book *Offbeat Kentuckians* may call to mind Charles Bramble, a rich and eccentric farmer of Cynthiana, Harrison County, who made plans to be buried in a limestone coffin full of Kentucky whiskey. He had to be buried in an ordinary wooden casket when his body would not fit in the sarcophagus. A well-to-do Kentuckian, Stephen Langford of Clay's Ferry, Madison County, attempted to do the same but with more success. Many years before his death, Langford prepared to have his remains hermetically sealed in a 1,800-pound coffin cut from stone in a Rockcastle County quarry. He had seen the horrifying sight of an improperly buried corpse that had been exhumed and eaten by groundhogs and he was determined that the same should not happen to him. Langford died on September 1, 1898, at age eighty-six, and throngs witnessed his stone coffin being dragged on a sled by four mules to its grave on a hilltop on the Langford farm.

Another Madison Countian who opted for a homemade sarcophagus was Ephraim Mitchell of Kingston, who was reported in 1901 to have ordered a one-ton stone coffin made of Rockcastle County granite. His motive was fear of grave robbers.

Organ Donor

George Cecil of Elizabethtown, Hardin County, donated an organ to the Valley Creek Church. Not long afterward, on August 31, 1908, he committed suicide by swallowing carbolic acid in the same barn where his father had hanged himself several years before. The first time the new organ was used, it played a funeral dirge for its donor.

Strader's Will

C.M. Strader of Louisville died in Philadelphia on March 6, 1904. The day before he joined the choir invisible, he wrote a will that included the following request: "When I am dead my wish is that my body shall be cremated. Then I will that my ashes shall be placed in an urn and taken back to Louisville, my birthplace and the home of my boyhood, and there scattered upon the waves of the beautiful Ohio river. When this is done, if the Angel Gabriel can collect my remains for the judgment, I will take off my hat to him and will be there at the last roll-call."

Just Like One of the Family

William Y. and Ada Hansbrough, a childless couple who lived at 403 West Chestnut Street, Louisville, certainly loved their dog, Billy, an intelligent but mischievous canine. In late

April 1905, about a week before his demise, Billy ran away from home and went on a "spree." His worried owners notified the police that Billy Hansbrough was missing and offered a twenty-five-dollar reward for his return. The authorities were somewhat nonplussed to discover that Billy was a terrier, not a boy. Billy's wanderings turned tragic when he took a lordly stroll down Fourth Avenue and saw something he evidently had never seen before: a bed of lime spread out on a construction site. As Billy observed the tempting shiny whiteness of the lime, his curiosity got the better of him and he started rolling around in it as if it were mud or a fragrant pile of sheep offal. The lime stuck to his skin and fur and he returned home looking more like a walking piñata than a dog. The alarmed Mrs. Hansbrough called a doctor, who gave her some bad advice: wash it off with water. When the water reacted with the lime, it "ate into [his] skin, then into his vitals, and he passed away in pain" on April 22, at age eight, surrounded by friends and loved ones.

The dog's owners were so grief-stricken that they held a wake. They called in an undertaker, who took Billy back to his parlor and embalmed him with as much care (and expense) as if he were a human. The Hansbroughs also published an obituary, complete with a photo. The funeral was held on the morning of April 24, after which the couple had Billy's remains taken by hearse to the family plot in Cave Hill Cemetery. Billy was laid to rest in an expensive casket; his owners assuaged their grief by visiting the grave site daily and bringing flowers. They moved out of their house within a fortnight, since they could not bear to live where they had raised their beloved Billy from a puppy.

There was a problem. When the Hansbroughs had asked to bury the dog in their plot, the majority of Cave Hill's board of directors agreed on the condition that "there would be no mound or marker," but the mourners violated the agreement by raising a mound and were said to be planning to put up a monument as well. Other plot owners objected to Billy's presence, saying that it trivialized the grief they felt for their own dearly departed.

The issue led to a legal battle that continued for more than two years. One plot owner in particular, Henry Hertle, felt so insulted that a dog should be buried nearby that he spearheaded a lawsuit filed in chancery court in January 1906 against W.Y. Hansbrough and the Cave Hill Cemetery Company, in order to force them to exhume Billy and dispose of him. The grounds of the petition were threefold: firstly, Hansbrough and the cemetery were "guilty of keeping and maintaining a nuisance." Secondly, the cemetery's charter stated that it was intended for "deceased white persons," and Billy was manifestly not a member of this select group. Thirdly, the plaintiff, Mr. Hertle, was "greatly humiliated in thinking that the bodies of those who were near and dear to him lie near the buried dog and in the contemplation that of the probability that when he dies, his body will also be buried beside that of a dog." One wonders just what Hertle had against dogs, anyway.

It seemed at first glance that Hertle had a legally airtight case. On the other hand, Cave Hill's charter did not explicitly say that animals could *not* be buried there and it would not be easy to prove that a long-dead and deeply buried dog could be a "nuisance." One of Hertle's attorneys, Merit O'Neal, remarked that as far as his firm could tell, the case was without precedent. The Cave Hill Board of Directors said that they were perfectly willing to have Billy removed, but of course the Hansbroughs would have none of it.

On March 30, 1907, after more than a year of legal jousting, Chancellor Miller ruled that man's best friend could stay put. "If the claim of right here asserted be permitted to control," said Miller, "it would prevent the burial of anyone—a murderer or a suicide, for instance —whose grave might be objectionable to neighboring lot owners. That matter is in control of the cemetery company. An unburied dog, either alive or dead, may be a nuisance, but a dead dog, well buried, as in this case, is not a nuisance, and cannot become one."

Miller threw the case out of court, but Hertle was stubborn and had the decision appealed. The circuit court's decision was overruled by the state court of appeals in December 1907. In the words of the ironically named Judge Barker:

> *If the body of a dog may find sepulchre on the lot of its owner in Cave Hill Cemetery, why might not the owner of a horse, or bull, or donkey, also bury his favorite on his therein, if his fancy should take this freakish direction? Where would or could the line be drawn if not at the body of a dog? We believe the average man*

*would consider it an outrage on his rights as a lot owner
in a cemetery if the owner of an adjoining lot should
inter the carcass of a dog beside the lot which holds the
grave of his family.*

And with this final decision, I assume, Billy Hansbrough was disinterred and taken to a more congenial burying ground. According to cemetery records, William Y. Hansbrough is buried in Cave Hill, but not his wife Ada. It appears she took her business elsewhere.

A Gift of Questionable Taste

In November 1901, Mr. and Mrs. John Williams of Danville, Boyle County, celebrated their golden wedding anniversary. One of their friends, J.E. Wright, was a monument salesman and for a present he gave the elderly couple "a handsomely designed tombstone with the names of the couple engraved on it" to be placed on their plot in Bellevue Cemetery. Instead of beating Wright with their canes and throwing cake at him, as one might expect, the Williamses were reportedly "delighted with the unique gift."

Mrs. Brewster Gets Boycotted

Owen J. Owen (not a typo) Brewster, "a young lawyer, wretchedly poor," had the great misfortune to inspire the wrath of the morticians of Louisville. In 1891, his father died and he was unable to pay the undertaking firm, C. Miller's Sons, for the burial expenses, which amounted to fifty-two dollars. That was the first strike against Brewster.

The attorney's eighteen-year-old wife, Susie, died of heart disease on December 10, 1893. Tragically, the Brewsters had been married for only seven months. When the heartbroken husband went to the office of C. Miller's Sons to make the needful arrangements, he was archly informed by John Miller that the firm would *not* bury Susie since Brewster still owed them for his father's services. Not content with rebuffing Brewster, the Millers used their influence to encourage other undertaking establishments not to bury the corpse. John Miller claimed that the Funeral Directors' Association of the Falls Cities, known as the Undertakers' Union for short, had a rule that no bodies could be buried unless all the next-of-kin's outstanding bills were paid; he also threatened to "stop the funeral in the street" if Brewster dared to go to another firm. Miller was not bluffing: the union actually had such a rule and every funeral establishment in town except one belonged to the union. In effect, poor Susie was about to be boycotted.

After leaving C. Miller's Sons, Brewster took his business to a different firm: Mrs. George Ratterman and Son. They refused to help. Brewster then tried his luck with Mrs. D. Bax and Son, who had not yet caught wind of the controversy. In those days, embalming often was done at the residence of the deceased rather than at the funeral parlor, so L.D. Bax went to the home of Brewster's mother to do his work.

He got so far as to place Susie's body on a cooling board, but then he was informed of the boycott. He packed his bags, informing Brewster that he could do nothing until the matter was settled. Yes, the embalmer left Susie's body on the cooling board right there in the Brewster residence. When Brewster's mother asked Bax if he would be so kind as to take the remains with him, he replied with shocking tactlessness: "What are you worrying about it for? She's no kin to you." At least he had the common decency to throw a sheet over the corpse. There the body stayed, no doubt to Mama Brewster's annoyance.

By December 13, Susie was showing unmistakable signs of decomposition. The Brewsters opened the windows in hopes that the chill winter air would slow nature's processes. A couple of good citizens, Major Kinney and attorney Reuben Buckley, raised a fund to have Susie properly disposed of. With the money in hand, Brewster's sister Frances asked the firm of Schoppenhorst Brothers to take care of matters—only to be informed that union etiquette required that they could not remove the body until the original undertakers consulted, C. Miller's Sons, gave permission. The Brewsters got the same negative answer from William Watson, a black mortician. In frustration, Frances went to the Millers to pay them and beg their leave to have the decomposing body removed from her mother's house—but the Millers held a grudge and refused to either accept the money or grant the permission. Perhaps the reader will get some insight into why some people really don't care for unions.

Defeated, Owen Brewster gave up on having a stately funeral for his partner in life's sorrows and joys. He submitted to letting the city undertaker give Susie a pauper's burial in Cave Hill Cemetery as an act of charity—but even this official would not bury her unless a coffin were provided. Although sympathizers had collected a large sum of money with which Brewster could have purchased a beautiful casket, thanks to the union boycott he could buy none in the city. Susie was instead buried in a battered old walnut coffin donated by the University of Louisville Medical College and the Brewsters had to place the body in the coffin themselves. "One of the neighbors who was present said that he had never seen a more affecting scene," remarked a reporter. A hearse was provided by August Leffert, the only undertaker in the city who did not belong to the union. The burial took place on December 15, five long days after Susie's death.

When asked about the events by a reporter, John Miller did not deny they had happened, but he had a different spin on matters. He said that Brewster had refused several times to pay for his father's burial and Miller felt that he "was only protecting his business in demanding payment of the old bill before making a new one." In addition, the city's other undertaking firms confirmed that under union rules they could not have buried Susie Brewster without getting the Miller Brothers' kind authorization. The story made national news and, if an editorial which appeared in the (New York) *Commercial-Advertiser* is any indicator, public sympathy was with the Brewsters. "Business is business," thundered the paper, "but only people whose finer instincts have been wiped out by professionalism would attempt to block a man's efforts to get his wife's dead body underground."

But the story did not end with Susie Brewster's interment—of course not! In January 1894, Brewster, being a lawyer, decided to bring a lawsuit against the unreasonable folks at Miller's, several other undertaking establishments, the Louisville Coffin Company and the Undertaker's Union for $25,000. The modern equivalent of this sum would be precisely $577,981.65, and never mind the $0.65.

Like the Hansbroughs' lawsuit against Cave Hill Cemetery regarding the burial of their dog, Brewster's suit against the Undertakers' Union was unprecedented in American law. Obviously, Louisville has long been a trailblazer when it comes to the disposal of dead things.

On one hand, Brewster felt that the undertakers' behavior had been disgraceful and that his family had been subjected to humiliation and mental anguish; on the other hand, the union protested that morticians had to take drastic measures to protect themselves from deadbeats (sorry) who would request expensive services for their dearly departed and then refuse to pay. After all, buried bodies cannot be evicted from their plots and no one is willing to buy a secondhand, repossessed casket.

Some of the best legal minds in Louisville took Brewster's case pro bono. He won the first round, but lost when the suit went to the court of appeals, which had no problem with the undertakers of Louisville conspiring to leave a dead teenage girl in a private residence for five days, despite the health hazards posed and despite the fact that her family had managed to scrape up enough money for the burial.

Brewster died of consumption on December 14, 1902, at age forty-two. He appears to have been buried beside his wife promptly, with no muss and no fuss.

Treasure in Kentucky

The phrase "buried treasure" makes one think of states with an exotic history of mining for precious metals, such as California or Nevada, or states with a history of piratical shenanigans, such as South Carolina, Louisiana or Florida. Nevertheless, landlocked Kentucky has yielded its share of buried treasure. Most of it was hidden by misers who didn't trust banks or people who buried their money in secret locations during the Civil War and then failed to retrieve it.

For example, in February 1887, Sam A. Hill and Will Watkins of Marshall County were clearing ground near the home of Frank Gordon, about a mile east of Sharpe, when they found a sinkhole that, upon closer examination, turned out to be a sizable cave. Fifteen feet from the surface they found a room measuring twenty by thirty feet. It was filled with $600 in gold and silver coins, some silverware and, not incidentally, two human skeletons. Locals remembered that during the Civil War, the area had been terrorized by

Bloody Bill Brady and his guerrillas. In 1864, Union troops under Colonel Hackett had ambushed the guerrillas at Benton and killed all but two, who disappeared and never were seen again. Marshall Countians conjectured that the two had returned to the secret cave and killed each other in a dispute over the cache.

In 1896, John G. Leonard, who lived four miles from Harrodsburg, Mercer County, occupied himself by looking through papers owned by his recently deceased mother-in-law, Phoebe Schofield. Among them were letters written by her husband, John Schofield, who had joined the Union army after the Battle of Perryville and had been killed in the war. Leonard discovered a note written by Schofield to his family, in which he stated that he had hidden a box full of money near the family's house. He had buried the box five feet deep between two white oak trees about five feet apart and had marked the exact spot with a sharp rock. John Leonard went out exploring and found what seemed to be the location described: one oak remained while only the stump of the other remained. To his dismay, Leonard realized that he was physically unable to excavate the hoard himself. The understandably excited man then made two fundamental mistakes: he did not immediately hire diggers and he could not resist telling neighbors the secret. When Leonard finally got around to employing some laborers a couple of days later, he found that someone had beaten him to it. All that was left was a hole, at the bottom of which was a square shape indicating that a box had been removed from the earth. Moral: If you find directions to hidden treasure, keep it to yourself.

Another example of a Kentucky treasure that may or may not have been found originates from Petersburg, Boone County. On the morning of February 18, 1908, a stranger calling himself Jefferson Hawkins greeted Magistrate Solon Early by stating that he had spent some time in the penitentiary at Frankfort. While there, said Hawkins, he had become acquainted with an elderly murderer named Williams, who confided to Hawkins the location—which happened to be on Early's property—where he had buried $15,000 stolen from a bank years before. After Williams was sent up for murder, he never had a chance to salvage his ill-gotten loot. Hawkins showed Early a map allegedly drawn by Williams and made a suggestion: "Let me dig up the treasure and I'll give you $5,000 of it," or words to that effect. Early agreed and the two dug several holes in the general location indicated by the map, only to find naught. Early went to sleep that night convinced the whole thing was a practical joke, but the next morning his nephew Earl Walton informed him that a brand new hole had appeared overnight a few hundred yards from the dig site. At the bottom was a "well-defined imprint" shaped like a box. Early later discovered that a man fitting Hawkins's description had been seen that morning boarding the Cincinnati, Lawrenceburg, and Aurora train.

Charley Wells of Mayfield, Graves County, successfully found an unexpected trove. Around 1908, while excavating for a sawmill near Woodville, McCracken County, he uncovered an iron kettle filled with more than $5,000 in old gold and silver coins of peculiar shape. A firm specializing in rare coins in Cincinnati purchased the entire bonanza for

$9,000. Wells traveled extensively out West, but despite his temporary good fortune his life ended sadly. Wells caught typhoid in Paducah in summer 1909; as a result he went insane and in February 1910 was committed to the Western Kentucky Asylum at Hopkinsville.

In many instances, Kentucky treasure was found by sheer happenstance. On June 20, 1901, the eleven-year-old son of John Crews, a farmer who lived four miles east of Princeton, Caldwell County, was plowing a field when he uncovered a half dollar. Excited, he and his little sister continued digging in the vicinity until they had turned up between $350 and $400 in coins that dated between 1811 and 1845. They also found part of an old boot that likely had once held the coins. An old-timer claimed that a tree had once stood on the location where the children found the money.

While plowing the garden in early June 1904, Mayfield farmer J.A. Jackson and his son found several hundred dollars in gold and silver coins with dates that ranged from 1842 to 1860.

On April 6, 1907, Oscar Prichard of Cannonsburg, Boyd County, was excavating for a new house on a site where there stood a house in antebellum times. His labors were rewarded when he found six skeletons lying side by side, between two of which was $300 in gold coins, all predating the Civil War.

In April 1907, farmer John Miller found a skeleton while digging for saltpeter in a cave belonging to J.S. Harlan at Glasgow, Barren County. Work was halted for a few days, but on April 26 explorers discovered an empty pot, "some mutilated jewelry which appears to have belonged to an Indian" and "some writing…in an unknown language." On the same evening, some anonymous person in Tompkinsville had sold some old coins in excellent condition that dated as far back as 1746. Perhaps it was a coincidence, but many assumed that the mysterious coin seller had beaten everyone to the cave and found riches others had missed.

Strangely, the very next day—April 27, 1907—more treasure was found in Shelbyville, Shelby County. A stonemason named John Jones found a rotten cedar bucket containing $1,800 in gold coins while prying up an old stump.

A truly remarkable find was made in February 1909 by H.S. Hensley and Albert Pawley as they wrecked the old Nathan Ross house near Paint Lick, Garrard County. When they removed the hearthstone, they found $22,500 in gold and silver coins, $3,000 worth of diamonds, a revolver and several thousand dollars in Confederate money.

In late March 1909, Mrs. L.C. Gooch purchased a lot on Colfax Street in Lexington, Fayette County, for $116; she was more than remunerated when, on April 8, two workmen named James and Leslie Cox unearthed an old metal cooking pot with a brass cover that contained $805 in gold and silver coins. (To put it in terms of modern currency, that would be the equivalent of spending $2,650 and getting back $18,400.) No one knew who had hidden the money, but the likeliest suspect was a ten-years-deceased Civil War veteran named Dewitt, who had been the lot's previous owner. He had lived in a squalid shanty on the site for thirty years.

W.B. Mastin of Millersburg, Bourbon County, dug up a rotten wooden box in his garden in May 1910 that held $200 in silver coins minted between 1720 and 1888. It was thought to have been buried by the previous occupants, an eccentric miser named John Padgett and his sister. Similarly, while plowing his father's field in August 1910, a young farmer named David Coursey of Spa, Logan County, unearthed a box with "contents as good as new"—$500 in gold coins and some undisclosed "valuable papers."

On June 3, 1910, George Keller, a Garrard County blacksmith, while diving in the Dix River near King's Mill, found a pine strongbox on the river bottom. After retrieving it, he found that it was in such poor condition that one end was entirely missing. But it still contained part of a tantalizing treasure: three five-dollar gold pieces and three five-dollar gold coins, all dated before the Civil War. Presumably, the rest of the money was scattered along the riverbed and may still be there. An elderly citizen named E. Flaig recalled that the area had been infested with gangs of bank robbers in the days before the war. Years later, a thief on his deathbed in Lexington had confessed that his gang had robbed a bank in Nicholasville and had thrown the box containing their loot in the river near King's Mill while a posse was in hot pursuit. That seemed to solve the mystery.

In some cases, buried swag was found via mystical means. Around 1899, a gypsy fortune teller told J.E.S. Ott, who lived near Danville, Boyle County, that someday he would dig up a treasure. The prophecy came true on July 15, 1901, when Mr. Ott was hoeing his garden and uncovered an old wooden box containing 1,600 silver dollars. Another lucky man, John Vandiver of Rockport, Ohio County, had a dream in July 1907, in which he found money hidden in a hollow tree on his farm. The dream was so realistic that Vandiver sought out the tree. It enclosed a tin can with $3,000 in gold coins and greenbacks.

Some treasure may still be waiting to be discovered. It had been rumored for years in Clay County that $11,000 in gold and silver coins lay buried somewhere by a miser known as "Madcap." Allegedly, two strangers found the treasure in March 1901, near the point where Hector Creek empties into Red Bird Creek, but the story cannot be confirmed. Near Roberts Station in Henderson County, on the Green River, there was a cave commonly called the "Buzzard Hole" that served as a community hiding place for valuables during the Civil War. Twenty years after the war, the property on which the cave was located belonged to William Vaughn. He seems to have had a curious lack of interest in exploring the cave, but one who did, George Fryor, found a large rock a short distance from the entrance. When he turned it over he found a note that read:

> *Plotters Cave, Apr. 20, 1868.*
> *Entrance to cave:—Go in 100 ft., turn to right-hand and go through a room, enter a vault, turn to the left and go through another room, at entrance to room you will find a small door, which open and you will find our treasure. Given to finder.*

The note was signed "M.N.P." Naturally, Fryor attempted to follow the directions, but found to his dismay that the cave had been closed up and he could get no farther in than forty-eight feet. Mr. Vaughn expressed interest in excavating, but there is no record that he did so. Was the treasure ever found? Was it simply impossible to get to? Or was the whole thing a practical joke? One wonders why the curiously generous "M.N.P." never took the treasure for himself.

Random Strangeness

Bibles in the Wall

William Gullett and his wife Nannie lived in the Rome district near Stanley, Daviess County, for over fifty years. When William died around 1904, his widow inherited "a considerable fortune." She immediately began spending the money in mysterious ways that unnerved the community. First, she moved out of her house and into a cabin three miles below Stanley, in an isolated area some distance from the highway and the railroad. Then, she hired a contractor from Louisville to construct a building near her cabin. Sometime in the fall of 1906, a workforce of laborers arrived on the scene and started building one of the largest and most expensive houses ever constructed in the area. By the time it was finished in winter 1907, it was three stories high and "of ample length and breadth." To most people it resembled a school building, but Mrs. Gullett and her contractor refused to tell anyone what it was for. A few rather creepy details leaked out: some of the rooms were furnished with school desks and inside a niche in one wall Mrs. Gullett placed a bushel's worth of Bibles, which her workmen then sealed up. The elderly widow was a Christian Scientist, leading some to believe that the mysterious building was intended to be a school for Christian Scientists.

Mrs. Gullett died on April 10, 1918, at age seventy-nine. Her will bequeathed one hundred dollars a year for ten years to the Christian Science Church of Owensboro, but unfortunately it provides us with no clue as to the purpose of the strange building she had constructed.

Entombed Animals

In September 1883, Nath Deatheridge of Richmond, Madison County, was hard at work making a cistern. After blasting down to a level of fifteen feet below the surface, Deatheridge found that he had broken off a rock so large that it could not be brought whole to the surface. He climbed down into the hole with a stone hammer and commenced crushing the rock. One blow split the rock in half and out jumped a frog which had had been imprisoned in a hollow spot in the center for who knows how many centuries. Deatheridge released the frog in his yard and for the next several days he saw it "hopping about as lively as if he had lived only sixty days instead of 60,000 years."

A similar but less dramatic incident occurred near Ashland, Boyd County, in November 1885. When an air shaft of the Williams Creek tunnel on the C&O railroad was opened for the first time in four years, someone found a securely sealed tin lunch bucket. The bucket, when opened, was found to contain a live ground snake over a foot in length. A news correspondent wrote: "How the snake got there, how long he was a prisoner, and on what it subsisted, are questions agitating many of our citizens."

Flying Man Over Louisville

A famous Kentucky incident turns up in several books on the paranormal, most influentially in Charles Fort's 1931 work, *Lo!* In the late nineteenth century, several respectable (that is, presumably not drunk) citizens saw a man operating a flying machine over Louisville. Newspaper reports from the period seem to confirm that people saw *something* strange in the sky, if not necessarily what they thought they were seeing. Some writers on the supernatural consider the tale of the flying man one of the earliest confirmed sightings of a UFO.

The first article on the subject appears in the *Courier-Journal* of July 29, 1880, with a less-than-serious headline: "More Monkeying Between the Talented Reporters and That Well-Preserved Old Dame, Madame Rumor." The article relates that C.A. Youngman and Ben Flexner saw the machine flying overhead as they stood by Haddart's Drugstore between six o'clock and seven o'clock in the evening of July 28. They thought they saw a man operating the machinery within: "He worked his feet as though he was running a treadle, and his arms seemed to be swinging to and fro above his head, though the latter movement sometimes appeared to be executed with wings or fans." The drugstore's proprietor, Haddart, also saw the flying object; he was described as having a "good character for veracity." The July 30 edition informs us that Haddart's was flooded with curiosity-seekers who wanted to hear all about the flying machine, including "two nimble correspondents of Eastern papers." A woman claimed that she and her husband also saw the "aeronaut," and the druggist is quoted as telling a scoffer: "[W]e saw it, and I wonder that it was not noticed by others."

On August 6, the paper reprinted a letter by Dr. D.F. Dempsey from the *Madisonville Times*. Dempsey claimed that a few witnesses in Madisonville had seen an unidentified flying object even before they read the *Courier-Journal*'s report. The doctor claimed that a local family, the Roysters, and several children saw something strange in the sky at sundown on July 28: "[Mr. Royster] said there seemed to be a ball at each end of the thing, and it looked as if it was about over the depot. It sometimes appeared in a circular form and changed to an oval."

On September 5, the *Courier-Journal* reported that the machine had made its way farther east and had been spotted over New York City. An article reproduced from the *Brooklyn Argus* stated that "a queer looking object" recently had been seen in the sky over the southern end of Gravesend: "It was not at all like a balloon, and not more than one-fourth the size of an ordinary balloon. It was black and resembled an immense bug in appearance more so than anything else. It had four arms or legs, which were operated by the occupant with a motion very much like that of a turtle when swimming." It appeared to be heading for Staten Island or Keyport, New Jersey. The Louisville witnesses had only thought they saw a man inside the machine, but the Brooklyn witnesses were more certain:

The face of the occupant could be seen looking down from the forepart of the machine and it looked as though he was in the position of a person swimming, with the machine above him and fastened close to his body. Just as he passed the point where the New York and Brighton

Beach railroad passes over the Prospect Park and Coney Island railroad, a train on the latter road came along and the engineer blew his whistle, to which the flying man responded by flapping his arms vigorously.

The then-respectable *New York Times* got into the act, running an editorial about the phenomenon. Many writers on the paranormal practice deception when they quote the *Times*, for they reprint only the editorial's first paragraph:

One day last week a marvelous apparition was seen near Coney Island. At the height of at least a thousand feet in the air a strange object was in the act of flying toward the New-Jersey coast. It was apparently a man with bat's wings and improved frog's legs. The face of the man could be distinctly seen, and it wore a cruel and determined expression. The movements made by the object closely resembled those of a frog in the act of swimming with his hind legs and flying with his front legs. Of course, no respectable frog has ever been known to conduct himself in precisely that way; but were a frog to wear bat's wings, and attempt to swim and fly at the same time, he would correctly imitate the conduct of the Coney Island monster. When we add that this monster waved his wings in answer to the whistle of a locomotive, and was of a deep black color, the alarming nature of the apparition can be imagined. The object was seen by many reputable persons, and they all agree that it was a man engaged in flying toward New-Jersey.

The impression one gets from the paragraph is that the editorialist is waxing amazement over the monster, which "was seen by many reputable persons." The piece gains credibility by virtue of having appeared in the *New York Times* in the days before America's foremost newspaper became an organ for Stalin apologists, reporters who are pathological liars and editors who expose secret programs designed to fight the nation's enemies during wartime. But occultists rarely quote from the rest of the lengthy editorial, because then the article's tongue-in-cheek flavor would become evident. The *Times* was making fun of the monster, but one would never guess that when those few choice snippets are presented. The editorialist goes on to suggest that the creature must actually be a scientist who has solved the mystery of flight but who has refused to reveal his secret because he is "engaged in some undertaking which he cannot safely proclaim." Perhaps he was "an aerial criminal, a fact which explains the cruelty and determination visible on his countenance."

On the other hand, the *Times* suggested, perhaps the flying man was T. DeWitt Talmage, a celebrated New York City preacher who had just returned from the West, where he had been "in search of entertaining local varieties of crime wherewith to embellish his sermons." The *Times* being the *Times*, the writer could not resist tweaking St. Louis and Kentucky by noting that the strange object had recently been seen there because they were "precisely the places which might be expected to yield a rich reward to an investigator of crime." (On the same day the editorial sneering at crime rates in other states was published, the *Times*'s "City and Suburban News" column included a squib that began: "Last week the police arrested 1,502 persons." The column went on to recount tales of counterfeiting, burglary, swindling and barroom fights.) The writer concluded that Talmage must have been flying over Coney Island to see what sins were being committed on the beach. The facetious *Times* editorial was the last word on the man who allegedly had conquered flight over twenty years before the Wright brothers.

It is impossible to state with authority what these people saw in the sky over 120 years ago, but there is probably less to the story than meets the eye. We must not overlook the comic tone the newspapers took, which indicates that the reports were not taken seriously. (Many modern writers on supernatural topics overlook or choose to ignore this elemental fact. The author of a paperback from the 1960s called *Strange People of the Unknown* boldly theorized that the flying creature from 1880 must have been an ancestor of "Mothman," the monster that terrorized Point Pleasant, West Virginia, in the mid-1960s—yet most reports on Mothman agree that he was a hairy, ill-tempered winged critter who flew without the aid of machinery, not a gadget-bound humanoid with frog legs. The author wrote that the Coney Island monster was spotted "in later years" at St. Louis and Kentucky—although the *Times* editorial makes it clear that the monster was seen in those places about a month *before* it entertained New Yorkers. The author also claimed that hundreds of people saw the flying man when neither the *Courier-Journal* nor the *New York Times* provide such inflated numbers. To compound these sins, the author of *Strange People of the Unknown* also took excerpts from the *Times* editorial and passed them off as firsthand quotations from eyewitnesses.)

There are reasons other than contemporary ridicule to doubt that the witnesses in 1880 actually saw a man or monster flying through the atmosphere. Only a tiny handful of people out of thousands of potential witnesses in Louisville and New York (and all states in between, for that matter) claimed to have seen the machine, and it appears that no Louisville paper other than the *Courier-Journal* reported the sightings. Since the machine was allegedly spotted over Madisonville, the *Madisonville Times* perhaps could have provided us with clues, but unfortunately no issues from that year exist. The *New York Times* editorial mentions that the object was seen in St. Louis, but a search of microfilmed papers yielded no corroborating news reports. Whatever the people saw, it apparently was first seen flying over Kentucky skies.

We must also wonder at the discrepancies in descriptions given by eyewitnesses. Louisvillians thought they saw a man working a flying machine with his hands and feet; the Madisonville spectators did not report seeing a human form at all, but rather an amorphous object that changed shape from circular to oval and appeared to have a ball at each end; in Brooklyn, people saw a black four-armed machine that resembled a bug with a man inside; and the *New York Times*'s detailed account noted that the man seemed to be decked out with frog legs and bat wings and that he wore a "cruel and determined expression," which witnesses could somehow discern though he was flying a thousand feet above the city. Unless more evidence surfaces, we can only wonder what the observers saw, but one thing is certain: the technology for a hand-cranked lighter-than-air machine did not exist in 1880.

Window Weirdness

In July 1882, the *Cincinnati Enquirer* reported on the eccentricities of a window in the two-story log farmhouse of Jesse Stith, who lived six miles west of DeMossville, Pendleton County. Specifically, a picture of a rainbow was imprinted in the window. According to Mr. Stith, it had appeared mysteriously just after a severe storm at the end of the Civil War. The neighbors were afraid of the cheery picture, as they were convinced that it was some arcane harbinger of evil. According to the reporter, "The rainbow is about six inches broad and reaches from one side of the window to the other, involving all of three panes of the lower sash, the colors from the top downward being orange, red, purple, blue, green, yellow, violet—blue and green varying somewhat from the natural gradation of the colors of the rainbow." The rainbow could be seen only from the outside, was visible from up to fifty yards away, moved with the window whenever it was opened, and could clearly be seen from the Portland Road; thus, it attracted the attention of many an appreciative wayfarer whose soul responded to beauty. The story was confirmed in Mildred Bowen Belew's local history *Pendleton County, the First 200 Years*.

The community of Milford, Bracken County, was agog in the summer of 1887 when pictures of professional artistic quality were somehow imprinted on the windowpanes of houses. The phenomenon first manifested itself at the home of William Showalter. One day he noticed that his windows had unaccountably turned "the colors of the rainbow." Two days later, portraits of people and various animals were visible in the glass. As if this were not marvel enough, pictures began appearing in the windows of several of Showalter's neighbors within a radius of two or three miles.

One of the strangest things about the pictures was their utterly random subject matter. At one house, a window was graced with a portrait of a man resembling Abraham Lincoln. At another, the drawings included a young girl bending over an infant, the number twenty-two, a lion and a landscape. One window featured a complete rendering of Noah's ark, while another depicted a drunkard. A reporter who visited the scene reported with ill-concealed astonishment that "the half had not been told," adding that each house so favored was visited daily by hundreds of vaguely terrified sightseers, "many of whom are awe-stricken and fearful that something terrible is about to take place…The people of Bracken County have not in years been more worked up over anything than they now are over these pictures."

The pictures turned out not to be harbingers of disaster for the community, but people were still left with the task of explaining the origin of the drawings. Some attributed them to the sun's reflection in water; others thought it was the moon's doings. Neither explanation made a dram of sense as heavenly bodies are not noted for having artistic skills. The most logical solution is that some roving artist or practical joker etched the pictures in glass with, say, a diamond ring. But this would be an excruciatingly time-consuming prank and very risky once the alarmed citizens started keeping watchful eyes on their windows. Further difficulties for the skeptics' standard one-size-fits-all practical joker explanation are that some of the pictures were rendered in navy blue and vivid crimson, and "gleam[ed] on the glass like a bright reflection." Elaborate pictures even appeared on the securely shuttered windows of the Milford Baptist Church. At last report, the pictures were starting to appear on windows in Browningsville, several miles from Milford. Then all news of the strange and unasked-for artwork ceased. Perhaps somebody took photographs that will surface one of these days.

Comparable weirdness occurred fifteen years later in Greenup County. In August 1902, there came a sensational report that hundreds of people had tramped out to the ridge between Schultz and White Oak Creek in order to gaze at the window of a long-abandoned log cabin in which the faces of the dead appeared "as plainly as they ever saw them in life." A contemporary wrote, "[T]he picture of one person will appear and remain for a few minutes when it will fade away and another will appear." The images were so lifelike that some viewers felt moved to speak to the faces in the glass. James Howland, Mrs. Jonas Harr, Jennie Glenn and Ella Lee were among the recognized dear departed citizens who appeared in window portraits.

Atmospheric Irregularities

It sometimes happens that people scanning the heavens see things they do not expect to see. We are concerned here not with UFOs but rather with unusual, though evidently natural, phenomena—such as the strange display over Henderson County one night in February 1896. According to the *Henderson Journal*:

> *A strange light was seen directly in the east which lasted half an hour or more. Just above the horizon the sky was a glowing red, above for a brief space was darkness and still higher a bright red streak shot upward what seemed to the eye a hundred feet. The light was apparently about two feet in width and was a very bright red and well defined. Many who saw it say that they never saw such a thing before.*

It would be tempting to call the red glow and the sharply defined red streak tricks of the setting sun, but they appeared about a half-hour before midnight.

At noon on February 27, 1898, some residents of Beaver Dam, Ohio County, saw a rainbow "that had the nerve to back up against the sun." That night, an even stranger sight was visible from Louisville. As described elsewhere in this book, the good and patient citizens of that city had in the past been pelted from above with lizards, salamanders, water beetles, quails, martins, bluebirds, grasshoppers, worms, frogs and fish. As if that were not enough heavenly persecution, Louisvillians who happened to be up after 8:00 p.m. got to see the universe's latest prank. As described by the *Courier-Journal*:

> [The moon] *was first surrounded by a small circle, and then there was the segment of a second circle that made a magnificent sweep around the zenith. The large circle cut the little circle in two, and when they finally faded away a little before midnight they were followed by a well-developed Grecian cross with the moon in the*

center…It was when the cross appeared over the face of the moon that the telephone bells at the newspaper offices rang the liveliest, although they had been jingling at a lively rate all night.

Many terrified observers interpreted the phenomenon to mean the end of the world was at hand. Since the battleship *Maine* had exploded in Havana Harbor a couple of weeks before, others felt that it was a sign of an impending war with Spain. Some wiseacres "suggested that the sun's flirtations early in the day aroused the moon to [have] a little fun on her own account."

A little less than a month after the lunar eccentricities observed in Louisville, the town of Richmond in Madison County received a shower of sulfur two nights in a row. It had the genuine article's characteristic aroma and was flammable; reportedly, a few other towns, including Mount Vernon, received it, too. No one had any idea where it came from, but since Richmond was under a smallpox quarantine at the time, some residents believed it was a disinfectant sent from Heaven.

A generation earlier, on the night of March 12, 1867, various parts of the state, including Bowling Green (Warren County) and South Union (Logan County), were afflicted with yellow rain. The event was noteworthy enough to rate a mention in *Scientific American*.

Paris, Bourbon County, was the site of some natural psychedelia on May 28, 1907. A contemporary news item is worth quoting in its entirety:

A remarkable exhibition of astronomical phenomena, witnessed by hundreds of citizens, was seen in the heavens here this morning. The sun, which was shining brightly, was surrounded by a large, brilliantly colored circle enclosed by another, both showing all colors of the rainbow. The outer circle was broken at short intervals by what appeared to be bright, round spots. Midway between the two circles irregular masses of light-colored clouds floated, while the rest of the sky was clear and blue. At the [Louisville and Nashville] *passenger station hundreds of waiting passengers viewed the strange spectacle, while trainmen left their trains and gazed in wonder. None was able to offer a satisfactory theory.*

In January 1918, early rising Mercer Countians got to see a patriotic vision of a mysterious flag in the sky. The *Harrodsburg Herald* described it as

a large blood red banner in the sky, that in a few moments changed to the semblance of a flag with the white bars across it. The banner was low above the northwestern horizon and appeared between four and five o'clock in the morning. Those who saw it state that it was about 300 feet in length and wide in proportion. It moved with a slow majestic sweep eastward and disappeared…It was too early in the morning for the sun to lend any color to the sky, and [the vision] *being in the northwest, was also an evidence that the sun*

could have been in no way responsible for the luminous
banner.

On April 9, 1919, eastern Kentucky was subjected to a shock that appeared to be an earthquake, but actually was a meteor entering the earth's atmosphere. Professor A.M. Miller of the University of Kentucky, hoping to find its resting place, made a public plea for information from anyone who saw it. The meteorite was discovered at Cumberland Falls in Whitley County and turned out to be so unorthodox that, in the words of the journal *Nature*, "if the object had not been seen to fall, its meteoric character would not have been suspected." It was a "meteoric breccia"—that is, it was made of two different types of stone melded together, one light and one dark, unlike the conventional, unadventurous meteorite. A Mr. G.P. Merrill thought it was a fragment from an exploded planet. Some scientists thought it had a terrestrial origin, that it was "an earth-born meteor expelled in a mighty eruption in long-past ages." A professor named Sampson suggested that it was a wayward piece of the moon.

You Don't Have to Go to Hell
Unless You Want To

A famous story about Calvin Coolidge originates from early in his political career, when he served in the Massachusetts Senate. When a senator angrily told Coolidge to go to hell, the future president calmly replied: "Senator, I've looked up the law on that and I don't have to go."

Little did Coolidge know that a variation on this delicate point of law had already been determined decades before in Kentucky. A Methodist meeting had been held in Owsley County, during which the minister asked rhetorically whether anyone in the congregation actually wanted to go to the fiery pit. A wiseguy in the back row held up his hand. This sarcastic act bothered onlookers so much that they had the smart aleck indicted for disturbing the peace. He was tried at the end of January 1891 by a circuit riding judge named Boyd from London, Laurel County. Sworn witnesses described the scene and the defendant admitted that he had raised his hand after the preacher asked the question. Judge Boyd's official decision was that, "to his knowledge, the code of Kentucky did not contain any law preventing a man from going to hell if he chose to."

The Tooth Vomiter

It all started in January 1895 when Fannie Thompson, the thirty-five-year-old pregnant wife of James E. Thompson, a black barber in Louisville, was about to get off a streetcar. The car moved before she had completely stepped off; as a result, Mrs. Thompson fell hard to the pavement. She received internal injuries and gave birth prematurely. For the next three months, she vomited quantities of blood every day. On April 17, the physician who cared for her, Dr. E.D. Whedbee, found that Mrs. Thompson had thrown up a small tooth that resembled a dog's tooth. She told the incredulous doctor that she had indeed vomited the tooth and had even felt it scratching the lining of her throat as it worked its merry way upward.

The good news was that from that point, Mrs. Thompson no longer vomited blood. The bad news is that she commenced throwing up teeth, or at least toothlike substances, at the rate of one or two a day. After a while, the teeth became bigger and looked like they had come from dogs, alligators, cows, hogs, horses, sheep and humans. By April, she was expelling between four and fourteen daily. They were described as being "merely thin shells and…filled with flesh." Dr. Whedbee, realizing that he was witnessing something unique, collected the teeth and preserved them in alcohol.

A number of prominent physicians in addition to Whedbee came to see Mrs. Thompson, including Drs. Flexner, Grant, Palmer and Samuels. They suspected Mrs. Thompson had been collecting teeth at slaughterhouses, swallowing them and then intentionally vomiting them —why exactly she would do this except for the joy of it or the publicity value, no one could hazard a guess. But despite careful surveillance, no one ever caught Mrs. Thompson swallowing the teeth of her fellow creatures. On the night of July 25, she threw up a half-dozen teeth within thirty minutes, all in the presence of Dr. Whedbee. A local paper thoughtfully provided a description of these odd impedimenta: "One of them looked like a horse's molar and had six prongs, four of which were broken off. It had the appearance of a tooth that had seen service and was about the size of the first joint of the thumb of a well-developed man. Another was about two inches long and very sharp at one of the ends. It curved like a hook." On another occasion she discharged five or six teeth within twenty minutes as Dr. Grant watched.

Mrs. Thompson threw up the teeth in the afternoon or evening, and always in the presence of a doctor since she was afraid one of the little grinders might choke her on the way out. She was able to throw them up at will, and yes, it hurt like the devil.

Symptoms that accompanied her strange ability—one could hardly call it a talent and certainly not a gift—included a constant pain on the left side of her stomach. Doctors noted a hard tumor-like swelling just below the left side of her ribcage. Digested food never came up along with the teeth, but they were accompanied by "a glairy mucus, very much like saliva," as though vomiting teeth weren't bad enough in itself.

Dr. Flexner chemically analyzed some of the four hundred putative teeth that Mrs. Thompson had disgorged, but the results were never announced and thus were likely inconclusive. The doctors also announced plans to put Mrs. Thompson under chloroform-induced sedation in order to examine her abdominal walls. However, when Drs. Grant, Rodman and Flexner showed up at the Thompson residence on July 26, she refused to allow the procedure on the grounds that she was afraid she might die while unconscious. She vomited five more teeth while she was at it.

Dr. Grant publicly announced that he thought Mrs. Thompson was pulling a hoax. He felt that she suffered from a peculiar mania that induced her to swallow animal teeth and then heave them back up. The teeth showed signs of having simmered in stomach acid and Dr. Grant theorized: "The woman swallows them perhaps several hours before she knows that it is time for her doctor to call on her, and is prepared to throw them up on short notice." The doctors announced plans to take her to an infirmary and isolate her in a room where no confederates could smuggle teeth to her and then see whether she still chundered the choppers.

The press does not state whether they followed through with this plan and, if so, what the results were. However, indications are that nothing positive was learned, for three years later Mrs. Thompson was still suffering from her bizarre affliction, despite having been subjected to "every experiment known to the medical profession." In January 1898, the *Courier-Journal*—which for some reason called her "Mary Lytle"—reported that she was living in fear of medical students, whom she felt would stop at nothing to solve the mystery. Allegedly, students loitered about her home and on two occasions even attempted to abduct her. Her relatives even applied to the chief of detectives and asked on her behalf for police protection. If she had faked the whole thing, she gained little from it.

Whole Lotta Shakin' Goin' On

A strange phenomenon, though probably not without an explanation, interested Louisvillians in the summer of 1894. The residents of two adjoining houses located at 1207 and 1209 West Jefferson Street were plagued with shaking furniture. The eastward half of the house was occupied by the G.W. Haas family—the W.J. Ryan family lived in the western half. All was a perfect delight until May, when both families noticed that their dressers "seemed to have taken life." On one occasion, Mrs. Ryan placed a pitcher of water on her dresser, only to have it fall off as though it had been pushed by an invisible hand. The families noticed that the metal handles on the dressers would constantly move up and down, making an irritating clicking noise. As time went by, the handles swung harder and the racket grew louder. The mirrors atop the dressers vibrated constantly.

Superstitious persons might have blamed the occurrences on a poltergeist, but the families were certain there was a natural explanation. To their annoyance, they could not find one. They thought perhaps heavy wagons passing by in the street caused the house to vibrate, but investigation proved that it shook even when the street was empty. In any case, the house had a solid foundation and had been constructed with a double layer of bricks, so outside traffic should not have shaken the building's contents to such an extent. Then the families thought the culprit might be electricity. They had the electric fire alarm wires removed from one of the house's two chimneys. The dressers shook anyway—and the situation got worse, for then the occupants could feel the floor shaking. Yet the phenomenon was silent except for the rattling made by the dresser handles. Grasping at straws, the Ryan and Haas families noted that an iron pipe leading from the house touched a streetcar pole, to which supporting wires were attached. Perhaps that could be a source of furniture-shaking electricity? This theory was tested and also found invalid.

Within a couple of days after the story hit print, the shaking had increased. Observers noted that decorative acorns hanging from one dresser rocked back and forth continually. Chairs moved, doubtless to the consternation of people sitting on them. "The motion seems to be a lateral one, from east to west," wrote one witness, "and objects on tables or shelves keep moving slowly to and fro. The vibrations number about 156 to the minute."

Matters took an even stranger turn when other houses in the vicinity of Twelfth and Jefferson began vibrating, too. People in the neighborhood claimed they could hear a constant hum or buzz, even late at night when the streets were deserted. Two medical men on the street, Dr. Dunn and Dr. J.T. Crecelius, felt the vibrations shaking their office and home, respectively. Neighbors heard the bell at nearby St. John's Episcopal Church ring faintly on occasion. The most commonly held theory on West Jefferson Street was that the strange shenanigans were the result of an underground electric current from some unknown source. A less scientific hypothesis held that the vibrations were the manifestation of ghosts from Baxter Square, which was once a cemetery. The Ben Schackhouse family was so unnerved by the constant shaking that they moved overnight after one daughter claimed to have seen a spirit rattling her window.

Dr. D.T. Smith investigated and decided that the vibrations were caused by the Daisy-line powerhouse at Tenth and Rowan Streets. The building was constructed on rock which transmitted vibrations to nearby houses. It seemed a tidy solution, but one venerable citizen pointed out that if this were so, then the vibrations should occur only during the powerhouse's hours of operation. Instead, the shaking occurred at all hours of day and well into the night. The citizen further stated that in 1889, before the Daisy-line powerhouse had been built, he had lived in a similarly pulsating house on Walnut Street, much farther west in the city.

The mystery apparently was never solved, but appears to have ceased of its own volition. The matter was dropped by the press and then forgotten.

The Marvelous, Though Absurd, Talking Trees

In 1862, a man was murdered under a tree located near Heath, McCracken County. Afterward the tree gained a reputation for being haunted. People reported that a voice could be heard issuing from it, usually preceded by a mysterious crashing sound. No doubt the reader wonders what a tree would say if it could talk, but unfortunately only one of the tree's statements has survived into posterity: "There are treasures buried at my roots." It appears that nobody ever took shovel in hand to determine whether the tree spoke the truth.

One might dismiss the tree's apparent power of speech as being the work of a practical joker, but most such pranks have a short life. The joker loses interest, is caught or confesses for the sheer joy of feeling superior to his victims. However, the stories about the tree at Heath continued for decades. Wary citizens began giving the tree a wide berth, and one family who lived close to it was so frightened that they sold their farm at a loss and moved to Texas.

The talking tree achieved the apex of its publicity in the long-gone autumn of 1904, when stories of its doings were published in newspapers as far away as Pittsburgh. By then, the land on which it stood was the property of Will Albert. For several months, enormous crowds gathered every Sunday hoping to hear the voice emanating from the notorious tree. When a Paducah newspaper covered the story, the sub-headline cautiously noted: "This May Be a Lie, But Many Truthful People Are Willing to Swear to It." One day, several of "the most reliable citizens of the county" investigated the tree. For hours, they listened and heard nothing. Just as they got up to leave, they heard the crashing noise that allegedly signaled the voice's advent. The report of this incident frustratingly does not state whether the tree spoke after the attention-getting preface.

Curiosity eventually died away and today few persons have heard of the sensational story. Persons eager to seek out the tree and listen to its wisdom should be advised that it was reported to be dead in September 1904, killed by the curious crowd's "continuous trampling on the earth" surrounding it. Perhaps the spirit of the tree, if any, has taken up residence in a nearby oak or a mailbox.

The story of the talking tree has a Boyle County parallel. In fall 1896, a party of raccoon hunters was in the woods near Danville. They noticed that when they approached a certain old tree, their dogs whined and ran away, tails tucked firmly betwixt their legs. One man "heard the sound of a voice as if from some soul in deep distress." The assembled hunters recalled pressing business in Danville, as did their dogs, and they all hurried back to town. The next day, an elderly man told one of their party that the same thing had happened to him years before. He recalled that many years ago a man named Henderson had robbed and murdered a man named Louis Streat and had dragged his corpse to the base of the tree, where he covered it with dead leaves. Henderson had been arrested and taken to jail, but fled the country after someone paid his $5,000 bond and had never been brought to justice. Some Boyle Countians believed Streat's indignant ghost haunted the spot where his body had been stashed.

If the prospect of talking trees does not unduly strain the reader's credulity, perhaps a talking rock will. Such a thing reportedly was found in Larue County, on Possum Kingdom Ridge on Knob Creek. There sat a worn limestone rock about five feet by three feet and fifteen inches thick. One day, circa 1879, some locals decided they wanted to use the rock for some purpose, so they dug around it enough to place levers under it. The workmen managed to raise the stone a few inches when they heard a voice issuing from it: "Let me alone!" Thinking it was a practical joke, they continued with their work. The voice cried out the same plaintive plea for solitude. The men were scared, but they were not about to let a rock tell them what to do, especially a common limestone. After a brief consultation, they applied so much strength to the levers that they raised the rock about a foot. The stone said in a despairing tone of voice: "Let me alone. I harm no one, so let me alone." This time the men did as they were told and fled the site. Word soon got out and Larue Countians turned out in numbers to contemplate the mysterious talking rock. As of May 1881, when the story finally reached print, despite lots of brave talk no one had attempted to remove the stone again.

It may still be there, just waiting.

The "Weeping Tree"

At about the same time Boyle Countians were baffled by a talking tree, they also had to contend with a maple that refused to behave as trees ought. The woody perennial was located on the lawn of R.D. Bruce, five miles from Danville. About three o'clock in the afternoon of Friday, November 4, 1898— a dry, cloudless and rainless day—three gentlemen who happened to be standing on Bruce's porch saw water falling from the maple's branches and leaves as though a downpour were taking place. The mystified men investigated by walking beneath the tree, but found no source of the water. The shower ended after an hour. No rain had fallen in the vicinity for several days, so it was not old rain being shaken off by the wind. The press made a special point of mentioning the reliability of the witnesses. They were A.P. Bruce, a liveryman, and two farmers named Charles Woods and Ben F. Slavin.

There once stood, and may still stand, another tree that was the locus of strange precipitation on East Fourth Street in Maysville, Mason County. It was located in front of Hannah Curtis's house and she often remarked that when she died her favorite tree would weep for her. Her passing came on April 8, 1899, and the *Maysville Public Ledger* commented in its April 15 issue: "[S]ure enough there is a constant drip from several of its branches and has been ever since her death. This is no April fool joke, but an actual fact, as has been seen by quite a number of citizens."

A Tornadic Coincidence

On the night of March 27, 1890, just before 8:00 p.m., Louisville was struck by one of the most disastrous tornadoes in Kentucky history. The funnel was three hundred yards wide and traveled fifteen miles across Louisville and part of Indiana. Modern researchers have estimated that the tornado, which killed 120 people, measured an F4 on the Fujita scale. As is the wont of tornadoes, the high winds performed some grimly amusing tricks, if one puts aside the wholesale death and destruction. For example, the Louisville tornado securely jammed a bed's headboard in the crotch of a tree in the yard of Dr. J.T. Crecelius on Jefferson Street, between Eleventh and Twelfth Streets. (The doctor, of course, lived with another enigma a few later when his house constantly vibrated. Some guys have all the luck.) The headboard stayed in the tree for years.

On the night of March 27, 1900, about 8:00 p.m., the already-wary residents of Dr. Crecelius's neighborhood were terrified by a "crashing sound followed by a clattering, as if the tin roof of some house was being torn off." Rushing outside, they found that the old headboard had fallen seemingly of its own volition. It had fallen out of the tree exactly a decade after the tornado had deposited it there.

A Light Trips the Light Fantastic

"Doc" Teater of Nevada, Mercer County, lived in a very old house near Bethel Cemetery. One night in September 1902, Mrs. Teater saw "a bright light dancing like a weird specter over the organ" in a largely unused front room. She investigated, thinking that perhaps she was seeing the reflections of a lighted lamp in a mirror. She found the room totally empty of all light sources except for the dancing blob. She left considerably quicker than she entered and alerted the rest of the family with a few heartfelt screams. The entire Teater clan hurried to her aid and saw the hyperactive light. They, too, searched the room to no avail. They even pulled the curtains tight in case the phenomenon was a trick of the moonlight, but the light kept up its nimble midair jig. The neighbors were alerted and very soon a number of citizens were in the Teaters' front room gawking at the eerie sight. After a while, the glowing globe slowly moved upward while rotating and disappeared through the ceiling.

Two or three nights later, Mrs. Teater noticed light streaming through the keyhole of the front room. She wisely called for her sons to come open the door. When they did, they found the room "brilliantly illuminated with a colored light." Again, the family searched for lamps or other light sources and found none; again, the neighbors came and witnessed the events. Gradually, the light faded away until nothing was left but a "dazzling ball of fire." As before, the ball of light begged its leave by moving upward and passing through the ceiling, leaving the room pitch-black and full of scared people.

For the next several nights, the Teaters' house was the most popular residence in town. Neighbors came hoping to see the light for themselves and perhaps thence to explain its origin, but it appears that the light didn't return and their hopes for a tidy explanation were left unfulfilled.

The Bell Tolls for Thee

The Irish believed that the earsplitting shriek of a spirit called a banshee foretold the imminent demise of the member of a household. The family of Ben F. Crook, who lived in Kingston, Madison County, a hundred years ago, owned something that predicted death as accurately as a banshee, but which was more pleasant to the eardrums: a broken grandfather clock that chimed only when the Death Angel approached on swift, silent wings.

The details were given to the press by the Honorable R.H. Crook, a county attorney by trade and therefore not likely to pass his time with pointless fibs and nonsense. The antique clock had not worked since the early 1880s, but one day in 1891, it rang out one chime. A few days later, R.H. Crook's brother William passed away. In 1894, the clock again rang once and within a few days, Mr. Crook's mother died. In 1904, the clock rang twice and within a week the twins of Mr. Crook's sister, Mrs. Collins Yates, died on the same day. On the night of February 7, 1908, Margaret Crook heard the clock ring a single chime. Within five days, the Reaper had flown away with the soul of her stepmother. There is no record of the clock's further adventures, or whether it still exists, but it is probable that the Crook family found its music most unwelcome.

A Coroner Joins His Charges

In August 1874, Dick Moore was elected to the enviable position of coroner to the city of Louisville. Strangely, it appears that inspecting dozens of corpses each year in every conceivable stage of ripeness and form of violent remove may not have made Moore a happy man. He took a trip to Memphis, Tennessee, at the end of February 1878; on March 1 came news that Moore had become the responsibility of Memphis's coroner. One early telegraph stated that he had "accidentally killed himself"; a later message clarified that Moore died of a gunshot wound to the head in the cellar of Harvey Robinson's saloon, across the street from the Peabody Hotel. Even more specifically, he had died in a most undignified locale: sitting on the toilet in a public bathroom.

Moore's body was found with a revolver in its lap. It was never determined whether the cause of death had been suicide or a ghastly accident. On one hand, there were no powder burns on his face or in the wound, indicating that the gun had not been very close to his head when it fired. At the inquest, friends he had spent time with moments before his death said that Moore had been in good spirits—he had bought tickets to the theatre—and the last remark he had made was that he was looking forward to a visit from his wife and his mother. On the other hand, before going down to the cellar, Moore was seen pacing back and forth in the saloon several times, as though he had some weighty matter on his mind. Also, as the *Memphis Avalanche* noted, "How the pistol, lying as it was, could have sent an accidental ball at right angles into the brain is a mystery." Perhaps in deference to Moore's family, the Memphis coroner's jury ruled it an accidental shooting. Moore was laid to rest among his former charges in Cave Hill Cemetery.

But the story did not quite end with Moore's burial. Soon after his ignominious demise, the Memphis newspapers reported that the bathroom in which he died was said to be haunted. "Groans and moans have…been heard" issuing from the cellar, said one paper, "and on two occasions visitors have seen a human figure there acting in a strange manner." Gamblers who frequented the saloon were so convinced that a ghost lurked in the water closet that many of them refused to go there even in the daytime. Some of them thought they heard the sound of a pistol cocking preceding the moans and groans, and one swore that when he opened the bathroom door he beheld a man sitting with a bloody face and a hole in his right temple. Another witness, Joe Flynn, described as "a well-known river man," allegedly saw the ghost in the cellar although he had been unaware of Moore's death. Flynn even had a brief conversation with this unfriendliest of Caspers. In Flynn's own words:

> *When I went down it was tolerably dark, and I started to turn up the gas, when I heard a noise near the wall, and saw a large-sized man groping around. He kept putting his arms behind his back in a curious manner, and at last he whispered: "Get away from here." "Who are you?" I asked, and he said: "Never mind. You get out of here."…I was upstairs in about two seconds.*

Was Moore's ghost doomed to repeatedly reenact its untimely, violent death? Or did it simply wish to use the water closet? In either case, it seems the need for privacy extends into the afterlife.

The Belled Buzzard

One of the commonwealth's stranger legends concerns the fabled Belled Buzzard. For a decade or two in the late nineteenth and early twentieth centuries, a vulture with a bell tied around its neck was seen winging its way across Kentucky, alarming and amazing all who beheld it. Why anyone would want to bell a buzzard is a mystery in itself; perhaps it was for the ironic juxtaposition of the pleasant ringing of the bell mingled with the disgusting sight of the bird as it consumed carrion: music while you dine! The following is a list, by no means complete, of some Kentucky sightings.

John Meadors saw it on his farm near Big Spring, Breckinridge County, on April 14, 1883: "When noticed it was battling with two crows, and the bell made merry music for the fray." It made an encore appearance on August 25, 1886, when it was observed by Felix Sipes, who "was near enough to see the bell plainly," according to a contemporary account. "He says it is a round bell, and has the tone of a sheep bell."

In June 1883, the undertaker of the sky was seen over McLean County. The editor of the local paper, the *Progress*, made the journey from skepticism to belief: "We never believed the story…until we were told by the persons who participated in the fry across the river last week that they had seen it and had really heard the tiny ringing of the distant bell."

More than a decade later, in late April 1894, M.L. Fife of Hardin County saw everyone's favorite musical carnivorous raptor in his neighbor's wheat field.

D.P. Newman of Kevil, Ballard County, saw the buzzard on September 3, 1908. "I could hear it jingle 200 yards or more away when in the air," Newman wrote. "It has been many years since I heard it before." One of the buzzard's last documented appearances was over Pilot Knob, Simpson County, a couple of weeks before Christmas 1910.

So when, where and how did this bizarre creature originate? There are many competing legends. One theory is that at some point in the distant past, an unknown person belled a buzzard in order to frighten away all the other vultures in the area, thus possibly preventing the spread of communicable diseases. Another commonly accepted myth recounted in 1910 was that someone captured it in the early 1880s in Monroe County after a moonshiner named Anderson was shot to death in a gun battle with the sheriff and his posse. The connection between the two events passes the author's understanding, but perhaps someone with an idiosyncratic sense of humor belled the buzzard to commemorate Anderson's violent passing. However, the earliest account I have found appears in the *Courier-Journal* of April 15, 1883, in which an anonymous correspondent from Madisonville, Hopkins County, writes that Wash Rhea, "a very reliable man," reported recently seeing the buzzard flying over his farm. The correspondent added: "I saw an account several years ago of someone that belled a buzzard. I wonder if it is the same?" The fact that the legend was already "several years" old in 1883 rather demolishes the dead moonshiner theory.

Yet another conjecture about the bird's origin maintained that the vulture was captured by the sons of Samuel Ross of South Carrollton, Muhlenberg County, in 1873 or 1874. They tied "an ordinary sheep bell, with a thong of rawhide" behind the bird's wings and then released it in order that its lovely music might fill the air and gladden the hearts of all who heard it. The writer who sent this story to the *Courier-Journal* noted with a trace of nostalgia: "The buzzard was seen by hundreds of persons up and down Green River for thirty miles for months afterward. I have not heard of it for years."

A fourth theory came from Billy Trigg, an octogenarian of Corydon, Henderson County, who claimed in 1883 that he and a blacksmith friend named Hoffman had caught the buzzard in Pottsylvania County, Virginia, and given it

a brass collar with a small bell engraved with their initials back in 1823. If true, and if it were the same bird, the buzzard must have been at least sixty years old in 1883 —and it was seen sporadically for a couple of decades after that. The most likely explanation is that more than one person succumbed to the temptation to bell a buzzard and over the years a multiplicity of musical vultures were seen in various locations—a theory borne out by the fact that the bird was sighted in Indiana, Pennsylvania, Mississippi, Arkansas, Texas, Tennessee, North Carolina and probably several other states. That would explain both the buzzard's ubiquity and its amazing longevity. For example, a news article datelined December 29, 1887, claimed that a sharpshooter in Tunis, Texas, succeeded in shooting the buzzard, which wore a small brass bell with the year 1879 and three undisclosed initials engraved on it. But within a couple of weeks, a belled buzzard was thrilling easily entertained folks in the vicinity of Thyatira, Mississippi. In addition, the buzzard was reported to have frozen to death in Kentucky in the winter of 1910–11, yet was seen near Forest Grove, Clark County, in July 1911.

The idea that there was more than one buzzard was expressly stated by Kentucky humorist Irvin S. Cobb in his short story, "The Belled Buzzard," in which he also evokes the sense of awe the fabled bird inspired:

> *Once, years and years and years ago, someone trapped a buzzard, and before freeing it clamped about its skinny neck a copper band with a cowbell pendent from it. Since then the bird so ornamented has been seen a hundred times and heard oftener over an area as wide as half the continent. It has been reported, now in Kentucky, now in Texas, now in North Carolina now anywhere between the Ohio River and the Gulf. Crossroads correspondents take their pens in hand to write to the country papers that on such and such a date, at such a place, So-and-So saw the Belled Buzzard. Always it is* the *Belled Buzzard, never* a *Belled Buzzard. The Belled Buzzard is an institution.*

> *There must be more than one of them. It seems hard to believe that one bird, even a buzzard in his prime, and protected by law in every Southern state and known to be a bird of great age, could live so long and range so far and wear a clinking cowbell all the time! Probably other jokers have emulated the original joker; probably if the truth were known there have been a dozen such; but the country people will have it that there is only one Belled Buzzard a bird that bears a charmed life and on his neck an ever-silent bell.*

The Belled Buzzard—or, more likely, buzzards—made enough of a splash in the public imagination that someone wrote an Appalachian folk song called "The Belled Buzzard." Or perhaps the song came first and Kentucky's Belled Buzzard was the result of some demented music lover's attempt to bring the song's lyrics to life.

Paupers for Sale

When were human beings no longer sold like livestock in the United States? Almost everyone thinks such practices ceased in 1865, after the Civil War ended and Congress passed the Thirteenth Amendment to the Constitution, which officially abolished slavery. But it appears that few people have read the Thirteenth Amendment very closely.

Consider the case of John Hanson, a black vagrant sold into servitude at auction in front of the Louisville courthouse. Dick Zable, a vault cleaner, made the highest bid at two dollars (which suggests that nobody thought Hanson's services were worth very much). For putting up this princely sum, Zable had the legal right to own Hanson for the period of one year, "subject to the law which governs the contract between apprentice and master." Zable put Hanson to work tending to his horses. After the sale, there was serious talk of auctioning off a white vagrant named Mack.

So when did the auctioning of Hanson occur? On June 14, 1882—seventeen years after the passing of the Thirteenth Amendment.

Naturally, this did not escape unnoticed by the national press. Most papers roundly condemned the act—imagine, a person sold into servitude (albeit temporary) so long after the war!—but in fact, as the *New York Sun* pointed out, it was perfectly legal. "The recent sale," said the paper, "…has surprised many persons who were not aware or had forgotten that the Constitution of the United States distinctly recognizes the lawfulness of slavery or involuntary servitude as a punishment for crime."

Section One of the Thirteenth Amendment, ratified in December 1865, reads as follows (my italics): "Neither slavery nor involuntary servitude, *except as a punishment for crime whereof the party shall have been duly convicted*, shall exist within the United States, or any place subject to their jurisdiction." In other words, as the *Sun* put it:

There is nothing in the constitutional prohibition to prevent a State from making slavery the penalty for very trivial offenses. The fact that this has not been more generally attempted in the Southern States shows how the sentiments of the people have grown away from the old slave system. Besides, if a law was passed imposing slavery as a punishment on black culprits it would have to apply to white culprits also; and the possibility of a Negro owning a white slave would seem unpleasant to the ordinary legislator.

Hanson's sale was not the last time in Kentucky that a human was sold into servitude. The *Bowling Green Times* announced in late 1884 that Columbus Ford, "the most incorrigible and irrepressible colored vagrant in the state of Kentucky," would be sold at auction if he did not choose to stay in the county poorhouse. I am not certain whether the auction came to pass, but in June 1887, Mollie Jackson, a white pauper, was definitely sold to the highest bidder for thirty days at Paducah, McCracken County.

On February 9, 1895, the services of two black women, Sarah Jackson and Bettie Fishback, were sold at public auction at Georgetown, Scott County; the highest bidders were Henry Jackson and Richard Coleman, who, for a cumulative bid of $3.05, won the labor of the women for a period of six months. Newspapers from around the country, especially in the North, protested that the days of slavery had returned to the South—overlooking the fact that the men who bought the women's services were themselves black. The *Chicago Journal* called the auction "demoralizing." The *New York Advertiser* said, "Such trafficking in human flesh and blood should be stopped…[N]o person, black or white, should be permitted to be sold into servitude even for an hour." (The Northern press raised a similar outcry when two black vagabonds were auctioned at Lebanon, Marion County, in late October 1897.) The *Georgetown Press* responded to criticism of the sale:

> *Some of the philanthropists of the North are unnecessarily disturbed. Letters have been received asking if it is possible that the report is true. There is no need for unnecessary concern on the part of those tender-hearted people. There was neither oppression nor cruelty in the transaction. The women were street-walkers of the lowest class, and had they been consulted would doubtless have preferred to be disposed of in this way to confinement in jail. They had no money with which to pay a fine, and wouldn't work if it was offered to them. Some of the good people of the North would do an important favor to suggest some satisfactory plan for dealing with such characters.*

Several weeks later, in March 1895, another black vagrant, Sol Williams, was sold at the courthouse door in Paris, Bourbon County, for thirty-one dollars for a period of six months' servitude. But when an attempt was made to sell a pauper at Maysville, Mason County, in August, Judge Hutchinson ruled that vagrancy is not a crime and refused to allow the auction. In a similar incident, Josh Jones was due to be auctioned in Somerset, Pulaski County, in July 1900; he avoided the punishment only because the judge, T.Z. Morrow, like Judge Hutchinson at Maysville, believed the law was unconstitutional and "out of all proportion to the gravity of the offense."

Not every Kentucky official was so generously inclined, however; Deputy Sheriff M.H. Williams allowed the auction of a white hobo, Lawrence Peak, at the Elizabethtown courthouse in Hardin County on August 3, 1896. His purchaser, John Cecil, got six months' worth of work out of Peak for $12.75.

Arch Hays, a farmer who lived near Taylorsville, Spencer County, purchased at auction the services of a black vagrant, Sy Lewis, for nine months for only two dollars around August 6, 1901.

An interesting case occurred at Shelbyville, Shelby County, on September 6, 1902, when Sheriff R. Walter Briggs auctioned off a year's worth of servitude by Fisher Million, described as a "worthless Negro" who "enjoys the distinction of never having worked a day in his life." Perhaps the residents of Shelbyville were in no mood to be charitable with Million, since he had infected the town with smallpox in 1900, costing the city several thousand dollars in healthcare costs. The winning bid was made by David Murphy—who happened to be black—for a whopping four dollars. The well-respected farmer told Million that he would be treated well and would have plenty to eat and wear, but also vowed that he would make the hobo work even if he had to apply a whip: "Murphy afterward said he would have bid as high as $20 on the vagrant Negro. He said he bought him from a purely speculative standpoint, intending to make him work, and that no sentiment whatever governed him in making his strange purchase." Not only that, but an eyewitness reported: "Many Negroes attended the sale, and the fact that the vagrant was purchased by one of their color completely changed sentiment among them, and instead of mutterings which would have been the case had he been bought by a white man, the result meets with their hearty approval." For all that, Murphy soon received a threatening letter from a black organization at Hampden, Virginia.

On November 28, 1902, three black beggars—two women, Belle Griffin and Emma Reed, and a man named Charles Anderson—were sold at auction in Lancaster, Garrard County. Anderson's services were sold for seven dollars, while Griffin and Reed brought five dollars apiece. Anderson and Griffin were sold into servitude for one year, but Reed got three years.

Bruce Marcum, white, a "young, robust, and able-bodied man about twenty-seven years of age," was sold at public auction by the sheriff of Breathitt County on April 8, 1903. Deputy Sheriff Berry Turner "performed the duty with all the skill of a professional auctioneer, calling attention to the health and physical qualities of the young man, and impressing upon the crowd the value of the young man's labor." The winning bid for six months of Marcum's servitude was $6.50, placed by William Griffith.

Marcum was the nephew of attorney and United States Commissioner J.B. Marcum of Jackson, but his family connections did not save him from the auction block.

Another white male to be sold at auction was Dock Aubury of Meeting Creek, Hardin County, described as being "a strong, able-bodied man without means of support and too lazy to work." Aubury had recently gotten married and made the mistake of moving in with the bride's family and then refusing to work. When the in-laws got sick of his mooching, they instigated proceedings to have him tried as a vagrant. On December 3, 1906, blacksmith J.J. Johnson of Rineyville bought Aubury for one measly dollar before a large and sarcastic crowd. This means that Johnson got Aubury's services for a year at a cost of less than half a cent per day. "The town and county would be much benefited if more of such prosecutions were made against the worthless lot of loafers that can be found on the streets here at any time," remarked the *Elizabethtown News*. However, Aubury's servitude did not last long. On December 9, the judge ruled that the jury that convicted Aubury had been improperly instructed and the grateful pauper was set free. I wonder if he moved back in with his wife's family.

Lest anyone think the auctioning of hobos was strictly a Kentucky phenomenon, I have found cases of vagrants being sold at public auction in such places as Augusta, Kansas, in February 1887; Fayette, Missouri, on March 28, 1892; and in Lackawaxen Township, Pennsylvania, in January 1899. Undoubtedly, there are many more examples waiting to be discovered.

The clause in question remains in the Thirteenth Amendment. Does this mean you can be sold into slavery if you should become a pauper? Of course not—I think. Pay your debts on time; that's my advice.

Who Shall I Thank?

Rob Aken of the University of Kentucky Library; Ellen G. Ball, Berea College Archives and Special Collections; Geneta Chumley; Drema Colangelo; Jackie Couture; Eastern Kentucky University Archives and Special Collections; Eastern Kentucky University Department of English and Theatre; Eastern Kentucky University Interlibrary Loan Department; Lee Feathers; Ronda Foust; Rosie Garcia-Grimm; Dr. Jim Gifford; Kenneth Grimm; the Harrodsburg Historical Society; Hilary McCullough; Rene McGuire; Kyle and Bonnie McQueen; the Darrell McQueen family; Pat New; Colleen O'Connor Olson; Deonna Pinson; Gaile Sheppard; Michelle Steele; Mia Temple; the University of Kentucky Interlibrary Loan Department; John Wilkinson; and everyone at The History Press. Also: the Architect.

This book was edited by Lee Feathers.

Bibliography

For the Edification of the Curious

Kentucky Monsters

Bailey, Jack Dalton. *Murders, Mischief, Mysteries, Mayhem, Madness, Misdemeanors and Downright Meanness in Mercer.* Vol. 3. Harrodsburg, KY: n.p., 2005.

Brandon, Jim. *Weird America.* New York: Dutton, 1978.

Elizabethtown News. "Still Digging Out Curious Relics," November 18, 1911, 8.

Henderson Daily Gleaner. "Marine Monster," October 23, 1904, 12.

Louisville Courier-Journal. "A Beast or Man?" May 12, 1894, 5.

———. "Bird, Beast or Devil," October 12, 1884, 9.

———. "The Commonwealth," August 22, 1882, 4.

———. "A Curious Fish," March 16, 1899, 2.

———. "The 'Dog-Eater,'" February 9, 1885, 2.

———. "Eyes Like Fire," February 15, 1903, sec. III, 1.

———. "Graves Despoiled," November 12, 1909, 6.

———. "In and About Kentucky," November 28, 1887, 4.

———. "In the Grasp of an Unknown Animal…," July 24, 1903, 8.

———. "Kentucky News and Notes," September 26, 1899, 4.

———. "Kentucky News in Brief," June 22, 1903, 4.

———. "Killed the Varmint," October 31, 1889, 5.

———. "Mysterious Call of the Wild…," March 28, 1909, sec. I, 7.

———. "Out in the State," June 20, 1887, 6.

———. "Perhaps It Is Darwin's Missing Link," May 15, 1888, 2.

———. "Picturesque Life in Kentucky," April 11, 1897, sec. II, 6.

———. "Strange Animal," July 8, 1900, sec. II, 1.

———. "A Strange Animal," November 30, 1884, 4.

———. "What Is It? Mr. Ritman Would Like to Know," July 9, 1901, 6.

———. "The Wild Animal Known as the 'Dog Eater'…," March 27, 1885, 5.

———. "Wild Animal on the Rampage," June 18, 1896, 7.

———. "Wild Man Roams Over River Cliffs," March 23, 1907, 1.

———. "With a Grain of Salt," January 7, 1883, 9. Originally published in the *Richmond Herald*.

Meloan, Jack. "So You Thought Kentucky Had No Sea Monsters?" *Louisville Courier-Journal Magazine*, December 7, 1941, 13+.

Olson, Colleen O'Connor, and Charles Hanion. *Scary Stories of Mammoth Cave*. St. Louis: Cave Books, 2002.

Owensboro Messenger. "Eats Horses," September 30, 1904, 3.

———. "Maybe the Ohio Had One," September 8, 1904, 5.

———. "Mystery Surrounds the Drowning…," October 21, 1904, 1.

———. "Sea Serpent," September 8, 1904, 5.

Pinson, Deonna Turner. E-mail to author. June 16, 2006.

Stephens, Sam, ed. *Clark's Kentucky Almanac and Book of Facts 2006*. Lexington, KY: The Clark Group, 2005.

Ward, Joe. "Professor Says 'Monster' Swims in Herrington Lake." *Louisville Courier Journal*, August 7, 1972, A10.

Ward, John K. "Kentucky's Marine Monster." *Rural Kentuckian*, January 1985, 13–14.

A Vegan's Worst Nightmare Comes True

Fort, Charles. *The Complete Books of Charles Fort*. New York: Dover, 1974.

Louisville Courier-Journal. "Bath County's Phenomenon," March 13, 1876, 4.

———. "The Bath Wonder," March 22, 1876, 3.

———. "Blood Corpuscles," March 14, 1876, 4.

———. "The Fall of Flesh," March 11, 1876, 4.

———. "The Flesh Fall," March 20, 1876, 3.

———. "Out of Meat," March 17, 1876, 1.

———. "The Shower of Flesh," March 13, 1876, 1.

———. "The Shower of Flesh," March 16, 1876, 3.

———. "Startling Phenomenon," March 9, 1876, 2.

——— "That Flesh Shower," March 15, 1876, 3.

———. "That Shower," March 28, 1876, 2.

New York Times. "Flesh Descending in a Shower," March 10, 1876, 1.

———. "The Kentucky Meteors." Editorial, March 11, 1876, 4.

Scientific American. "A Shower of Meat," (March 25, 1876): 197.

Light Showers This Morning, With a Chance of Knitting Needles This Afternoon

Bailey, Jack Dalton. *Murders, Mischief, Mysteries, Mayhem, Madness, Misdemeanors and Downright Meanness in Mercer.* Vol. 1. Harrodsburg, KY: n.p, 2004.

Hartford (KY) Weekly Herald. "Miraculous Occurrence," September 27, 1899, 4.

Louisville Commercial. "A Plague in Louisville," July 21, 1882, 1.

Louisville Courier-Journal. "Another Shower of Plums," March 27, 1899, 4.

———. "Bath County Bugs," September 11, 1880, 4.

———. "Fish Fall," April 24, 1900, 2.

———. "From the Kentucky Papers," June 15, 1902, sec. II, 4.

———. "Home News," September 8, 1880, 1.

———. "It Rained Frogs," July 20, 1894, 6.

———. "A Mysterious Visitation," August 15, 1886, 14.

———. "One of the 'Bugs,'" September 9, 1880, 4.

———. "Remarkable Shower of 1856," March 13, 1903, 4.

———. "A Shower of Frogs," June 28, 1889, 8.

———. "Showers of Stones," July 28, 1886, 3.

———. "A Snake Fall," August 27, 1879, 4.

———. "A Strange Visitation," April 16, 1885, 3.

———. "Two Showers of Plums," January 31, 1898, 4.

Moseley, Frances B. Keightley. "The Disasters of Early Mercer County." *Mercer's Magazine*, September 1, 2005, 7.

"Odd Happenings Gets in News," No date, no publication, clipping courtesy the Harrodsburg Historical Society.

They Might Be Giants

Ball, Ellen G. E-mail to author, July 13, 2006.

Collins, Lewis and Richard. *History of Kentucky*, Vol. 1. Covington: Collins and Company, 1882.

———. *History of Kentucky*, Vol. 2. Covington: Collins and Company, 1878.

Elizabethtown (KY) News. "Tracks in the Rocks," February 10, 1870, 2.

Frankfort Tri-Weekly Yeoman. "The *Elizabethtown News* Says…," May 2, 1872, 3.

Lexington Dollar Weekly Press. "State Items," December 13, 1872, 6.

Louisville Courier-Journal. "Bones of Giant in Allen Discovered," July 31, 1925, sec. I, 4.

———. "Correspondents' Catches," January 20, 1885, 2.

———. "Dug Up a Giant," November 9, 1896, 1.

———. "Giants in Those Days," October 16, 1891, 1.

———. "The Giants of the Past." Editorial, December 28, 1911, 4.

———. "In and Around Kentucky," February 27, 1894, 4.

———. "Indian Giant's Skeleton Rests in the Morgue," July 17, 1901, 10.

———. "Kentucky News and Notes," April 23, 1897, 4.

———. "Kentucky News and Notes," August 20, 1897, 4.

———. "Kentucky News and Notes," May 8, 1897, 6.

———. "Large Skeletons Exhumed," December 11, 1900, 4.

———. "Matters in Kentucky," March 19, 1898, 6.

———. "Matters in Kentucky," January 31, 1899, 5.

———. "Other State Gossip," October 3, 1891, 6.

———. "A Prehistoric Giant Exhumed," November 25, 1877, 6.

———. "Queer and Odd Things in State Exchanges," April 25, 1897, sec. II, 6.

———. "Seven-Foot Skeleton of an Indian…," July 16, 1901, 7.

———. "Unearth Skeletons," April 1, 1910, 2.

Louisville Journal. "Giant's Bones," August 14, 1850, 3.

Steele, John Avroe. *Judge Rollin T. Hurt's History of Adair County, KY.* Edited by Michael C. Watson. Columbia, KY: Watson Publications, 1994.

Taylor, Harrison D. *Ohio County, Ky., in the Olden Days.* Louisville: John P. Morton and Company, 1926.

Young, Bennett H. "Col. Young Still Digging." *Louisville Courier-Journal,* August 20, 1894, 5.

———. "A Mound Explored." *Louisville Courier-Journal,* July 22, 1894, 4.

The Lexington Catacombs

Brandon, Jim. *Weird America.* New York: Dutton, 1978.

Ranck, George W. *History of Lexington, Ky.* Cincinnati: Robert Clarke and Company, 1872. Reprinted 1989 by Heritage Books, Bowie, MD.

Washington (PA) Reporter. "Kentucky Catacombs," December 4, 1872, 3.

Tales From the Graveyard

The Music Teacher's Last Request

Louisville Courier-Journal. "Piano for Her Bier," February 8, 1897, 2.

Macabre Practical Jokes

Lexington Herald. "Shroud Was Sent to a Dying Boy," December 29, 1905, 8.

Louisville Courier-Journal. "Frightful Greeting," January 4, 1897, 2.

———. "Grewsome Gift," December 28, 1905, 3.

They Got Lost

Lexington (KY) Dollar Weekly Press. "State Items," November 29, 1872, 5.

Bibliography

A Libel in Stone
Colangelo, Drema. E-mail to author, September 26, 2006.
Louisville Courier-Journal. "Epitaph," February 3, 1898, 5.
————. "Matters in Kentucky," March 12, 1898, 6.

Citizen Cane
Louisville Courier-Journal. "A Cane with a History," March 20, 1898, sec. I, 8.

Midnight Funeral
Louisville Courier-Journal. "A Burial at Midnight," September 10, 1898, 6.

The Convict's Grave
Louisville Courier-Journal. "Interesting Odds and Ends from the State Press," February 19, 1899, sec. III, 5.

Skeletal Surprises
Louisville Courier-Journal. "Bones Found in a Tree," March 23, 1899, 1.
————. "Crushed Skull," May 30, 1905, 3.
————. "Danville," January 24, 1903, 10.
————. "Kentucky News in Brief," September 7, 1903, 4.
————. "A Skeleton on File," November 16, 1902, sec. I, 5.
————. "A Strange Burial Place," August 30, 1889, 3.
————. "Weird Relic Obtained in Louisville," August 30, 1903, sec. V, 4.

Funereal Fisticuffs
Louisville Courier-Journal. "War Over a Funeral," April 4, 1899, 2.

BIBLIOGRAPHY

Three Graves, One Body

Louisville Courier-Journal. "Kentucky News in Brief," February 17, 1901, sec. II, 3.

Postmortem Pandemonium

Louisville Courier-Journal. "Signal Flag Falls and Sons Dig Up Father's Body," April 23, 1901, 1.

Taking Another Direction

Louisville Courier-Journal. "Wanted to be Buried with Head to the South," October 10, 1902, 1.

Three Long-Delayed Burials

Estep, Bill. "Legendary Cave Explorer Floyd Collins Reburied 64 Years After His Death." *Lexington Herald-Leader*, March 25, 1989, A1.

Lexington Herald-Leader. "Body Entombed in Cave Since '27 Might Be Moved," January 31, 1989.

Louisville Courier-Journal. "Remains of Baby are Finally Buried," June 19, 1904. Section I, 6.

McQueen, Keven. *Offbeat Kentuckians: Legends to Lunatics.* Kuttawa, KY: McClanahan Publishing, 2001.

Murray, Robert K., and Roger W. Brucker. *Trapped! The Story of Floyd Collins.* Lexington: University Press of Kentucky, 1982.

Death Warnings

Louisville Courier-Journal. "Another Prophetess Arises…," November 5, 1901, 8.

———. "Mrs. Peterman the Mysterious Prophetess," October 12, 1901, 3.

———. "The Remarkable Fate…," April 9, 1880, 4.

———. "Strange Case of Dr. Lemberger…," October 11, 1901, 7.

No Dogs Allowed

Lair, John. "Rockcastle Recollections: Buried Treasure." *Mt. Vernon Signal*, June 5, 1975.

———. *Rockcastle Roots*. Edited by J. Allen Singleton. Mount Vernon, KY: Polly House Publications, 1992.

Louisville Courier-Journal. "Matters in Kentucky," May 23, 1898, 4.

Langford's Sarcophagus

Louisville Courier-Journal. "In a Stone Coffin," September 3, 1898, 4.

———. "In His Stone Coffin," May 4, 1898. Section I, 3.

———. "To be Buried in a Coffin of Stone," July 25, 1901, 1.

Richmond Climax. "His Stone Coffin Weighed a Ton," September 7, 1898, 3.

Organ Donor

Louisville Courier-Journal. "Gives Organ to Church," September 2, 1908, 5.

Strader's Will

Louisville Courier-Journal. "Ashes Must be Scattered…," March 29, 1904, 1.

Just Like One of the Family

Louisville Courier-Journal. "'Billy' Hansbrough May Lie in Peace…," March 31, 1907, sec. I, 6.

———. "In Casket," April 24, 1905, 2.

———. "May Not Bury Pets Alongside Persons," December 19, 1907, 3.

———. "Object to the Dog," May 10, 1905, 8.

———. "Still After Dog," January 29, 1906, 2.

———. "Wants 'Billy Hansbrough' Removed," January 30, 1906, 10.

A Gift of Questionable Taste

Louisville Courier-Journal. "Tombstone Given as a Golden Wedding Present," November 27, 1901, 1.

Mrs. Brewster Gets Boycotted

Louisville Courier-Journal. "Against the Law of Decency," December 17, 1893, 10.

———. "Body Boycotted," December 14, 1893, 8.

———. "In a Second-Hand Coffin," December 15, 1893, 8.

———. "Laid to Rest at Last," December 16, 1893, 8.

———. "Sequel to the Brewster Case," January 7, 1894, 12.

———. "Wife's Body Lay Unburied for Many Days," December 15, 1902, 7.

Treasure in Kentucky

Louisville Courier-Journal. "Children Unearth Buried Treasure," June 22, 1901, 2.

———. "Digs Up Skeleton and $300 in Gold," April 7, 1907. Section I, 3.

———. "Dream Leads Man to Treasure in Tree," July 11, 1907, 1.

———. "Finds Gold Coins Valued at $1,800," April 28, 1907. Section IV, 10.

———. "Finds Old Strong Box in Bed of River," June 4, 1910, 1.

———. "Fortune Found Under Hearthstone…," February 26, 1909, 7.

———. "Gold and Silver Found in a Garden," June 5, 1904. Section I, 4.

———. "Gypsy's Prophecy Fulfilled," July 16, 1901, 4.

———. "Hidden Treasure," February 12, 1883, 1.

———. "Left a Big Hole in the Ground," February 20, 1908, 1.

———. "Matters in Kentucky," January 31, 1899, 5.

———. "May Have Found Pot of Buried Treasure," April 28, 1907. Section IV, 10.

———. "Mystery of Discovery of Gold Coins Solved," June 10, 1910, 7.

———. "A New Cave," February 19, 1887, 4.

———. "Plows Up Treasure Box," August 25, 1910, 3.

———. "Pots of Money Dug Up at Lexington…," April 10, 1909, 7.

———. "Treasure Trove Found in Bourbon County," May 29, 1910, sec. I, 6.

BIBLIOGRAPHY

———. "Two Strangers Reported to Have Found $11,000…," March 9, 1901, 3.

———. "Two Workmen Dig Up Pot of Money," April 9, 1909, 1.

———. "Youth Who Found Fortune is Insane," February 10, 1910, 5.

Random Strangeness

Bibles in the Wall

Louisville Courier-Journal. "Bushels of Bibles Sealed in Wall," February 4, 1907, 5.

Owensboro Inquirer. "Two Important Wills Are Filed," April 15, 1918, 2.

Entombed Animals

Louisville Courier-Journal. "A Frog Story," September 23, 1883, 7.

———. "A Winter Snake Story," November 26, 1885, 2.

Flying Man Over Louisville

Fort, Charles. *The Complete Books of Charles Fort.* New York: Dover, 1974.

Louisville Courier-Journal. "The Flying Machine," August 6, 1880, 4.

———. "The Flying-Machine," August 16, 1880, 4.

———. "The Flying Machine," July 30, 1880, 4.

———. "The Flying Machine East," September 5, 1880, 2.

———. "More Monkeying…," July 29, 1880, 4.

New York Times. "An Aerial Mystery," September 12, 1880, 6.

Tralins, Robert. *Weird People of the Unknown.* New York: Popular Library, 1969.

Window Weirdness

Belew, Mildred Bowen. *Pendleton County, the First 200 Years.* Holland Printers, 1994.

Georgetown Weekly Times. "A Rainbow as a Permanent Fixture…," August 9, 1882, 4.

Louisville Courier-Journal. "Pictures of Departed Appear in the Glass," August 22, 1902, 3.

———. "Pictures on the Windows," July 9, 1887, 4.

———. "Visions on the Glass," July 4, 1887, 3.

Atmospheric Irregularities

Bailey, Jack Dalton. *Murders, Mischief, Mysteries, Mayhem, Madness, Misdemeanors and Downright Meanness in Mercer.* Vol. 3. Harrodsburg, KY: n.p., 2005.

Louisville Courier-Journal. "Heavens Hold More Signs," March 1, 1898, 2.

———. "In and About Kentucky," February 20, 1896, 4.

———. "Night Owls," February 28, 1898, 8.

———. "Paris Sees Circles Around Old Sol," May 29, 1907, 2.

———. "Prof. A. M. Miller Studies Meteor," April 11, 1919, 6.

———. "Showers of Sulphur," March 24, 1898, 3.

Nature. "An Interesting Meteorite," 105 (August 12, 1920): 759.

Scientific American. "Yellow Rain," 16 (April 13, 1867): 233.

You Don't Have to Go to Hell Unless You Want To

Louisville Courier-Journal. "No Statute Against Going to Hell," February 2, 1891, 7.

The Tooth Vomiter

Louisville Courier-Journal. "Fears the Students," January 24, 1898, 2.

———. "Unexplained Mystery," July 27, 1895, 5.

———. "Very Strange," July 26, 1895, 6.

Whole Lotta Shakin' Goin' On

Louisville Courier-Journal. "The Furniture Still Shakes," June 24, 1894, 4.

———. "Matters of Common Talk," July 22, 1894, 10.

Bibliography

———. "Matters of Common Talk," July 23, 1894, 4.
———. "The Shaking is Spreading," June 19, 1894, 6.
———. "There Are No Ghosts But—," June 17, 1894, 12.

The Marvelous, Though Absurd, Talking Trees
Louisville Courier-Journal. "Elizabethtown, Ky.," May 27, 1881, 4.
———. "In and Around Kentucky," January 4, 1897, 4.
———. "Talking Tree," September 23, 1904, 4.
Paducah Daily News-Democrat. "A Mystery," September 21, 1904, 6.
Pittsburg (PA) Press. "Talking Tree of Kentucky," October 14, 1904, 6.

The "Weeping Tree"
Colaneglo, Drema. E-mail to author, December 19, 2006.
Louisville Courier-Journal. "Prediction Came True," April 24, 1899, 4.
———. "The Tree Wept," November 7, 1898, 2.
Maysville Daily Public Ledger. "Death's Doings," April 10, 1899, 1.
———. "There is a large tree…," April 15, 1899, 1.

A Tornadic Coincidence
Louisville Courier-Journal. "Caused a Scare," March 28, 1900, 2.

A Light Trips the Light Fantastic
Louisville Courier-Journal. "Weird Lights," September 15, 1902, 7.

The Bell Tolls for Thee
Louisville Courier-Journal. "Grandfather's Clock Tolls the Death Hour,"
    February 13, 1908, 1.

A Coroner Joins His Charges
Louisville Courier-Journal. "The Dead Coroner," March 4, 1878, 4.
———. "Dick Moore Dead!" March 2, 1878, 4.

BIBLIOGRAPHY

————. "Dick Moore's Death," March 3, 1878, 3.
————. "Dick Moore's Ghost," April 28, 1878, 3.
————. "The Last Rites," March 5, 1878, 4.

The Belled Buzzard

Louisville Courier-Journal. "The Belled Buzzard," January 4, 1887, 4.
————. "The Belled Buzzard Again," August 27, 1886, 1.
————. "A Belled Buzzard and Some Old Folks," April 15, 1883, 4.
————. "Belled Buzzard Makes Appearance in Simpson," December 14, 1910, 2.
————. "The Belled Buzzard Redivivus," January 11, 1887, 5.
————. "The Belled Buzzard Sighted," September 5, 1908, 6.
————. "Belled Buzzards," April 23, 1883, 2.
————. "The Commonwealth," June 11, 1883, 4.
————. "In and About Kentucky," May 7, 1894, 4.
————. "In Kentucky: There Are Dozens of Him," July 20, 1911, 4.
————. "That Belled Buzzard Again," November 19, 1886, 4.

Paupers for Sale

Louisville Courier-Journal. "Georgetown's Negro Vagrants," February 21, 1895, 4.
———— . "Human Being's Price is One Dollar," December 4, 1906, 2.
————. "Kentucky News," January 9, 1885, 7.
————. "Matters in Kentucky," November 2, 1897, 4.
————. "Negroes Sold at Auction," March 30, 1892, 1.
————. "Negro Farmer Purchases a Black Brother…," September 7, 1902, sec. III, 1.
————. "Negro Vagrant Will Be Offered For Sale…," September 5, 1902, 1.
————. "Odds and Ends of State News," March 21, 1895, 4.
————. "A Pauper Bids Herself In," January 11, 1899, 4.
————. "The Sale of a Vagrant," June 15, 1882, 6.
————. "The Sale of Vagrants," February 21, 1895, 4.
————. "Sets Aside Sale of White Man," December 10, 1906, 1.

———. "Shelbyville," October 4, 1902, 8.

———. "Slavery as a Punishment for Crime," July 12, 1882, 2.

———. "Taylorsville Vagrant Sold Into Servitude," August 7, 1901, 1.

———. "Their Services of Little Value," February 10, 1895, 3.

———. "Two Negro Women Sell For $5 Apiece," November 29, 1902, sec. I, 1.

———. "The Vagrancy Law," July 13, 1900, 4.

———. "Vagrancy Not a Crime," August 28, 1895, 1.

———. "A Vagrant Sold," August 5, 1896, 5.

———. "Will Sell White Man," November 26, 1906, 4.

———. "A Woman to be Sold for Vagrancy," June 4, 1887, 2.

———. "Young White Man Sold for Vagrancy," April 13, 1903, 6.

New York Daily Tribune. "Sold Into Temporary Slavery," June 4, 1887.

About the Author

K even McQueen is an instructor in the Department of English and Theatre at Eastern Kentucky University and is the author of seven books on Kentucky history. McQueen is also a leading authority on the mating habits of the dingo.

Other Books by Keven McQueen

Cassius M. Clay, Freedom's Champion
Offbeat Kentuckians: Legends to Lunatics
More Offbeat Kentuckians
Murder in Old Kentucky: True Crime Stories from the Bluegrass
Cruelly Murdered
The Kentucky Book of the Dead

For more information, go to kevenmcqueen.com.

Visit us at
www.historypress.net